CW01306689

joinanimus.com
Copyright © 2016 Mark Derian LLC
All rights reserved.

Man's Guide to Psychology

The integrated principles of consciousness and liberty

Written by Mark Derian

Edited by Ariana Kateri and Brian Gallagher

Against fatality, man has two weapons: consciousness and liberty.
– Victor Hugo

Introduction

To clarify the purpose of this book, here's a portion of my application essay for graduate school.

> The psychological field, perhaps because of its breadth and depth, is not yet a completed field like physics and chemistry. It is in the stage of observing and gathering material from which a future field will emerge. The current period of psychology is comparable to the pre-Socratic period of philosophy. As such, psychology has not yet found its Plato to organize its material and integrate its fundamental principles.
>
> I believe the integration of psychology and its application in the clinic will be the Platonic shift that transforms psychology from a fledgling to a fundamental philosophy. Carl Jung—who I consider to be the Socrates of psychology—is indispensable to the advancement of the field, but there are few, palpable models through which we can understand his ideas and how they relate to the rest of the field.
>
> It's my intention, therefore, to do for psychology what Plato did for philosophy—to explain the same number of phenomenon in fewer laws. The ancient Greeks were concerned with change and multiplicity, and so too are modern psychologists. What are the fundamental mechanisms behind psychological change, and how do they relate with other mechanisms in the psyche? This abstraction has been the course of advancement in all fields, and there's no reason psychology would be any different.

In other words, psychology has a ton of useful bits of information but few systems by which to make sense of and apply the information. There has been little attempt to unify psychological facts into a theory of what psychology is.

In the same way Plato unified philosophy into five branches—metaphysics, epistemology, ethics, politics, and aesthetics (and in the same way animals can be unified into seven branches—kingdom, phylum, class, order, family, genus, species) psychology can be unified into four branches.

Introduction

These four branches are anxiety, anger, identity, and self-awareness. They serve as the foundation by which we can understand consciousness. Every psychological disorder—and so every solution—can be boiled down to at least one of these branches.

Here's a diagram to illustrate how the branches of psychology relate with each other.

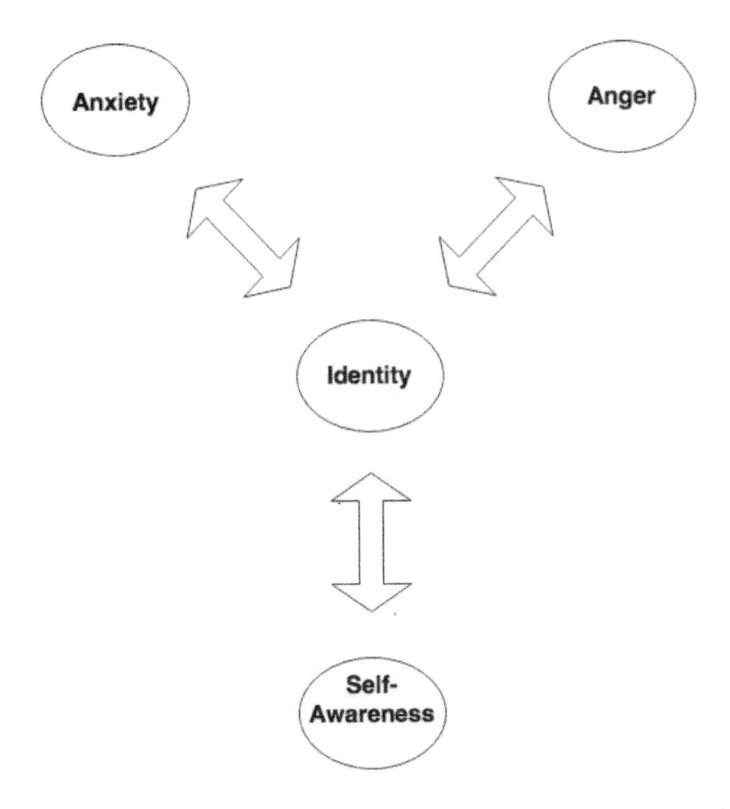

```
   Anxiety              Anger
        ↘              ↙
         ↖            ↗
            Identity
              ↕
          Self-
        Awareness
```

Anxiety and anger are at the top of the diagram because they are the least fundamental, and so most palpable, of the branches. Anxiety and anger are rooted in identity, which is more fundamental. And identity is rooted in self-awareness, the most fundamental branch of psychology.

Notice the arrows point in both directions. This indicates the flow of influence between the branches works both ways. Self-awareness affects identity, which in turn affects anger and anxiety. In fact, as self-awareness affects identity, it necessarily affects anger and anxiety. And any change in anger and anxiety necessarily affects identity and self-awareness in turn.

The Purpose of Psychological Unification

A unification of psychology into a system sounds nice, but why should we care?

To answer this question, let's take a step back. What are the surface-level qualities of the kind of man we want to be? The kind of man we all feel, deep down, we can be?

Here are a few I can think of:
- He's in control of himself and rarely loses his composure.
- He can handle any problem that comes his way, even if it sometimes means to forget about it and move on.
- He knows what he wants, and he can achieve it most of the time.
- When he sees a woman who he wants to meet, he talks to her.
- He can build a healthy relationship with a woman based on sexual chemistry and honesty.
- He may not be handsome, but he at least knows how to make himself look his best.
- He prefers peace, but he's comfortable with conflict.
- He has a positive effect on any environment.
- He introduces himself to strangers, and he introduces strangers to each other.
- He projects strength, even if he isn't physically strong.
- When other men are around him, they find themselves thinking, "Yeah, I need to be more like that."

Introduction

It's my contention that we cannot achieve any of these attributes through the focus of any single attribute itself. That would be a mere adoption of a new behavior when a new psychology is required. When we manage our deeper issues, these behaviors are the result.

This is why most guys have a difficult time with women and cannot improve their relationship with them no matter how hard they try. They think they need to do one thing as opposed to another. Make a certain approach, send a certain text, kiss her in a certain way, be a certain kind of guy. Their lack of a psychological foundation impedes their progress from step one. And if they do happen to push through and get some success, they're still seen as a joke because it's clear they lack a deeper maturity. Their issue with woman is only a symptom of a flawed psychology.

It's the same with alcoholics. The compulsive drinking is a symptom of a deeper cause. An alcoholic doesn't cure himself when he forces himself to put down the booze long enough for his sobriety to become a habit. This only works for a few weeks at most. He only puts down the drink fundamentally once he changes the psychology that causes the compulsion.

And I can do this with any other problem we may have. Procrastination, laziness, indecision, a sense of emptiness, existential dread, depression, suicidal thoughts, insomnia, poverty, codependence, obesity, isolation, stagnation. We are often unable to solve any of these problems if we focus on the problem itself. These are only symptoms of a deeper issue with our psychology. If we could solve one of these problems, say laziness, through the use of a technique we can find all over the internet, then by definition it wasn't a psychological issue. You've probably tried this already, which is why you picked up this book. You may think something's wrong with you, but nothing's wrong with you—the only problem here is no one has shown you exactly how your psychology works.

We can have all the sunlight and water and warm days we could need, but if our soil is desolate, the farm struggles.

Psychological unification is the fertile soil of the masculine man.

So I offer this: Once we get about 80 percent of each of the four branches of psychology handled, then the above attributes will take care of themselves—they will flow naturally and easily from our unified psychology.

That's the first reason psychological unification matters.

The second reason psychological unification matters is it makes it simple to conceptualize any problem we may have and understand how it relates to other problems.

There is no branch of psychology called "daddy issues." But there is a branch called "Anger." So if we're angry at our dad, it's not a problem with our dad, it's a problem with our anger.

There is no branch called, "I cannot believe my girlfriend broke up with me!" But there is a branch called "Anxiety," which teaches us how to deal with loss, and how this feeling of loss can transform into one of capability.

There is no branch called, "I always feel drained by the end of the day." But there is a branch called "Identity," which teaches us how to manage our time and energy, to only exchange them to benefit ourselves as well as others.

There is no branch called, "My life feels like it's flying by." But there is a branch called "Self-Awareness," which teaches us how to grab hold of the reins of our horse, to become more conscious of our thoughts and actions.

Psychological unification gives us perspective on our problems.

Our psychological issues may seem special to us, but they are all rooted in one of the four branches of psychology. I have yet to come across a psychological issue—from either the psychoanalytic or cognitive models—that doesn't fit into my unification.

Introduction

To paraphrase Carl Jung, the more personal a problem is, the more universal it is.

And to paraphrase me, the more universal a problem is, the more simple it is to overcome.

Table of Contents

Part I: Anxiety — 8
Chapter One: Avoidance — 13
Chapter Two: Helplessness — 20
Chapter Three: Confidence — 23

Part II: Anger — 36
Chapter One: Sadness — 41
Chapter Two: Hostility — 47
Chapter Three: Assertiveness — 53

Part III: Identity — 64
Chapter One: Mind — 68
Chapter Two: Decisions — 94
Chapter Three: Boundary — 101
Chapter Four: Individualism — 120

Part IV: Self-Awareness — 128
Chapter One: Theory — 133
Chapter Two: Practice — 151
Chapter Three: Application — 167

Conclusion: The Unification of Psychology — 184

Part I: Anxiety

How to become confident by understanding your anxiety.

"There is no such thing as duty.
If you know a thing is right, you want to do it.
If you don't want to do it—it isn't right.
If it's right and you don't want to do it,
you don't know what right is and you are not a man."
– Andrei Taganov

What Anxiety Is

Anxiety is a signal from our environment, represented as an emotional state, that tells us to avoid something. There is a threat, either existentially or psychologically, and anxiety is our body's adaptation to let us know this.

There are other words for anxiety. "Dread," "doubt," "fear," "regret," "discomfort," "concern," "panic," or "worry." But these words merely describe various shades of anxiety. We use language to tease apart the intricacies of our psychological states, but ultimately, it's all anxiety. And all anxiety, no matter how we describe it, is managed in fundamentally the same way.

Though anxiety is often labeled as a negative experience, this is only our perception of it. In truth, anxiety is nothing more than a signal from our environment that tells us to avoid something.

The Purpose of *Part I: Anxiety*

The purpose of *Anxiety* isn't to totally free our life of anxiety. Anxiety is a natural part of life, and it will continue to arise in different forms, and it will be triggered by different instances throughout life.

In fact, it is proper to feel anxiety. If we never feel any anxiety ever, then it means we don't challenge ourselves enough, or it means we're unaware of the anxiety.

Instead, the purpose of *Anxiety* is to help you master anxiety. This is the ability to turn anxiety into something useful. If you work with the information in this book, eventually you will get to the point where you see anxiety as a good thing because you will understand it as a herald of growth and masculinity.

Mastery of your anxiety can be difficult, like climbing a mountain. Fortunately, it's also simple, like climbing a mountain—keep putting one foot in front of the other and you'll get there. After all, there are only two causes of anxiety, and only three ways to handle anxiety.

Let's begin with the two causes of anxiety.

The Two Causes of Anxiety
In no particular order:
1. Loss, or the threat of loss, and
2. Avoidance of anxiety.

The loss can be any kind of loss. Loss of money, social status, self-concept, health, youth, family, or friends.

The avoidance of the anxiety is any anxiety-provoking situation you do not confront, whether it's avoided consciously or unconsciously.

Let's look at an example. You expect a large electric bill in the mail because it's been a hot July and you've left the air conditioner on more than usual. When the bill comes, it causes anxiety—it represents a loss of your money. Instead of paying the bill, because you cannot afford it, you leave it on the kitchen table unopened for a few days. When you avoid the bill, you implicitly tell yourself the bill is indeed a warranted threat, which only makes you feel more anxiety.

After a few more days, you may even tear the bill up and throw it away, with no plan to pay it in the immediate future. And since now you know you've incurred a late charge on the bill, you feel even more anxiety.

More fundamentally, anxiety builds due to a loss of your self-concept. Now you're the kind of man who turns away from his anxiety rather than confronts it.

Anxiety vs fear
Psychologists often make a point to distinguish between anxiety and fear. Anxiety is defined as a general sense of dread about no one, specific stimulus. Fear is anxiety about a specific stimulus. For instance, we feel fear about asking out a specific girl, but we feel anxiety about our relationship with women in general.

As far as I'm concerned, and as far as this book is concerned, there is no merit to this distinction. It adds unnecessary complexity. Anxiety is fear without awareness. There is always a cause of anxiety; you're simply unaware of the cause. To become aware of the cause of your anxiety is the first step in mastering it.

When you feel anxiety, it's essential to the management of the anxiety that you figure out what the anxiety signals—ie what in your environment causes the anxiety. Without first a realization of what the anxiety tells you, there will be no way for you to manage it.

Self-awareness is the first step in any change, which brings us to the first way to handle anxiety.

1. Avoidance—the Self-Destructive Way to Handle Anxiety

This is the automatic response to anxiety. It happens without conscious awareness. This is what the majority of men do when faced with a threatening situation. They simply avoid the situation, and then go on with their day.

It makes sense that our avoidance response to anxiety is the most common, because perhaps it's what humans have a proclivity to do. In Paleolithic times, when we regularly faced life-threatening situations, it was advantageous to our survival to act instantly without conscious awareness. When a saber-toothed tiger posed a threat, the self-aware types who cared more about how to manage their anxiety than survival rarely survived. The avoidant types had a better chance.

We come from a long line of men who were good at survival.

This avoidance impulse, however, doesn't serve us well today. Back to the example of the electric bill. An avoidance response would be to throw the bill away with barely a thought about it. It's how your ancestors dealt with the dangers of a saber-toothed tiger, so it's how you deal with the modern-day version of the saber-toothed tiger: money problems.

We may be inclined to perceive every threat as life-threatening, though today, only a few threats are.

Avoidance is great for survival, but it's unhelpful if we want to thrive. It neither dissipates the anxiety, nor uses it to your advantage. The anxiety not only remains, it grows with each act of avoidance. Your avoidance confirms, in your mind, the seriousness of the threat, and it confirms your inability to deal with the threat. The ten-foot dragon becomes a 20-foot dragon.

When you live years of your life in primarily avoidance mode, the anxiety completely envelops your psyche. Everything you do and say isn't done or spoken through you, but rather through your anxiety. Your thoughts and actions are no longer conducive to reality—rather, they're conducive to your perceived threat of reality. Every decision you make is no longer made by you—it's your anxiety that makes the decision. You become, quite literally, out of control. When you cannot handle the anxiety, the anxiety eventually handles you. Your life devolves into a random assortment of scenes you did not create, and you do not see coming. Chance is the driving force.

You don't even see what's happening because the anxiety covers its tracks and envelopes your psyche. You become the proverbial fish who doesn't know what water is, only for you the water is toxic.

To become aware of the anxiety caused and perpetuated by your avoidance, we therefore cannot look at your anxiety but rather the signals of your anxiety.

Here are the two signals of avoided anxiety:

I. Obsessive thoughts: Thoughts of an obsessive nature are when you effectively tell yourself "I can't." That's it. Every form of an obsessive thought can be boiled down to "I can't."

"I can't finish this project in time."
"I can't be who I want because of my poor upbringing."
"I can't get a girlfriend because I'm not handsome enough."

Worry and regret are the two most common forms of obsessive thought. Worry is anxiety over the future, and regret is anxiety over the past.

The source of your obsessive thought is often tricky to detect because what you obsess about is rarely the true cause of the anxiety. For instance, you may have obsessive thoughts about an upcoming move, and all that could possibly go wrong. But you've moved before, it's no big deal, and even if something does go wrong, you know you'll be able to manage it. Rather, the true cause of the anxiety comes from somewhere deeper in you psyche. It could be your destructive, cold relationship with your father. But to look at those issues with your father, and to confront them, is too difficult at the moment, so you displace the anxiety onto a manageable issue, like your upcoming move.

II. Compulsive behaviors aka "busyness": A compulsive behavior is any act you cannot stop in perpetuity with your own willpower. The shorthand is, if you try to quit something, but you cannot, then it's a compulsion. You may be able to quit for a while, but you revert to it. While the subtext of an obsessive thought is *"I can't,"* the subtext of a compulsive behavior is *"I have to."*

"I have to go to work today."
"I have to be nice to my girlfriend."
"I have to be muscular."

Often implied in the *"I have to"* is an *"or else."*

"I have to go to work today or else I'll get fired and be homeless."
"I have to be nice to my girlfriend or else she'll leave me and I'll be lonely forever."
"I have to be muscular or else I will never be good enough."

Compulsive behaviors are often linked with an obsessive *"I can't."* Hence, obsessive-compulsive.

"I can't talk to that girl but I have to or else I'll be a loser."

It reads like the dialogue in an indie movie.

What if you couldn't do something, yet you had to do that thing? Well, you would be in a state of constant action without getting anything done. You would be busy yet unaware of what you were doing.

Sounds like the plot of an indie movie.

Similar to obsessive thoughts, compulsive behaviors are rarely directed at the anxiety-provoking stimulus, because again, you likely doubt your ability to manage the anxiety-provoking stimulus.

You may focus your compulsion on the retentive organization of your kitchen utensil drawers, but you're not anxious about kitchen utensils. Instead, you may be anxious about your debt. *"I cannot pay off my debt,"* says the obsession, *"but I have to or else I won't be good enough,"* says the compulsion. So rather than face that issue, you work on an easier project, like the messy drawer.

Mindless internet use is a common example of compulsion. You come to a problem with work, and before you can even think about the problem, your mind skips right off to Youtube. You do it automatically.

Substance abuse and impulsiveness, or action without thought, are also common compulsive behaviors. These behaviors are momentary gasps for air as we drown in anxiety.

When we lack awareness, we live, act, and think in another world. It's a scary world because we are, quite literally, out of control.

Miscellaneous symptoms of avoidance include: lack of focus, insomnia, fidgeting, nail biting, hand wringing, panic, apathy, indigestion, muscle tension.

The full list of avoided anxiety symptoms is extensive, but these constitute what most guys experience. What's important to remember is any act or sensation that is involuntary, and cannot be controlled, is a sign of avoidance.

The portrait of avoidance

You wake up in the morning, and it begins even before your eyes open. "*I can't get up, but I have to.*"

You see a girl you want to meet, but before you even feel the anxiety of what it is to walk up and talk to a girl, you turn away from it. You tell yourself you don't even want to meet her.

You put your ear buds in and listen to music on your walk home in an attempt to disconnect yourself from the world. For reasons unknowable to you, you cannot focus, and you cannot sit still. You assume these are simply characteristics of who you are. You may think about it for a little bit, but you're only able to think about it through the anxiety itself, so you only experience a chorus of "*I can't's.*" The "*I can't's*" are real because anxiety is your reality.

Life becomes a series of distractions, like video games, entertainment, and alcohol. These are necessary for you because they make you feel okay with your dysfunction—according to your anxiety, there's nothing you can do about your dysfunction anyway. When in the state of avoidance, you are back in economy class, and the anxiety is your captain.

***

This is the portrait of the American male. He carries around a box of junk, yet he's unaware of it, so he wonders why his back is sore all the time. His anxiety controls him in ways he doesn't understand because he cannot see the anxiety. If you ask him about his anxiety, he would respond with, "*what anxiety?*" To him, this is what existence feels like. Just as the fish asks, "*what's water?*"

The way out of avoidance

The only way out of the avoidance of anxiety is to first understand the anxiety. Understand your obsessive thoughts, impulsivity, and avoidance behaviors are not you. They are anxiety's automatic responses.

Once you understand how anxiety has taken control of your life, you must allow yourself to *feel* the anxiety. Become aware of the anxiety. Make a list of what you avoid. Whenever a loss or threat of loss comes into your life—whether it's a loss of money, status, love, friendship—you must allow yourself to feel the anxiety of that loss.

When the large bill comes in the mail, open it, hold it, and feel the loss of it. When a girl scares you, get in touch with the fact that she scares you.

As you feel the anxiety, you are now more connected with reality.

Take an inventory of your anxiety. Write down all situations that could possibly be the cause of the anxiety. You can think of at least five, I'm sure. Then you'll have, at least your perceivable anxiety, there in black and white.

Once you become more and more comfortable with *feeling* your anxiety, without doing anything about it immediately, only then will you be able to think about the anxiety.

It's your job, as a mature man who must manage his anxiety, to first sit with your anxiety and figure out what it is telling you to do.

Of course, to sit with the anxiety is to be uncomfortable. But it becomes easier as we keep at it. Anxiety is nothing more than stress—it's a tension. It's like a 300-pound squat. This is difficult at first, to deal with the tension of the 300 pounds. As you submit yourself to increasingly heavier loads, you train your neuromuscular system to eventually squat 300 pounds. The process of anxiety management is no different.

I balk at what I implied earlier about how we are wired by evolution to avoid anxiety—not because it's incorrect, but incomplete. You may be built to deal with anxiety by avoidance, but you are not destined to deal with anxiety by avoidance. All men are more than capable of integrating their automatic responses to anxiety.

Let's say you're walking in the woods, and out of the corner of your eye you see a branch on the ground. But you perceive it as a snake. Before you can understand the branch to be what it is, certain parts of your brain take control and cause you to jump away in avoidance. This is indeed your wiring—you're built this way.

However, and this is crucial, you can expose yourself to enough of these situations and learn how to deal with a potential snakebite. With enough experience and knowledge, you develop comfort with the automatic response. When the automatic response becomes more comfortable, you can begin to feel the anxiety, and when you begin to feel the anxiety, you take the first step to overcome it. Even our two innate fears—ledges and loud noises—are manageable with enough awareness and exposure.

**Anxiety controls you in the short term,
but you control anxiety in the long term.**

Anxiety becomes easier to feel when you realize that, ultimately, though it may feel like a threat, it is not. It is merely a signal from your environment that tells you to avoid a threat. If you do not handle the signal properly, it will destroy you. But when you learn to handle the signal properly, you can use it for growth. The first step, though, is to feel the anxiety.

Once you learn to feel the anxiety, however, you can still handle it in an immature way, which brings us to the second decision we can make with anxiety.

2. Helplessness—the Destructive Way to Handle Anxiety

Unlike avoidance, helplessness is not a preconscious, automatic response to anxiety. You are aware of your anxiety, but you make an immature decision with it. In effect, you at least attempt to make other people manage your anxiety rather than manage it yourself. This is what I mean by "destructive"—you place the burden of your anxiety on the shoulders of others.

Helplessness may be destructive, but at least it's the step in the right direction away from the self-destruction of avoidance. When you're helpless with anxiety, you are at least look at the box of anxiety you lug around—you have become aware enough to know why your back is sore. Rather than manage the burden yourself, you dump it into someone else's box for them to carry, to make their back sore.

We do this because, ultimately, we see ourselves as unable to manage the anxiety on our own. Why else bother someone else with it? An attempt to place the responsibility of the anxiety on others feels like the only way to manage it.

Helplessness takes on many forms:

Complaints: When you complain to others, you effectively communicate to them, "*I am helpless to deal with this situation.*" This doesn't mean to never talk to people about a problem, but complaints only draw attention to the problem—it makes others focus on you in order to relieve your anxiety. This contrasts the healthier way to talk about your problems with the intention to both connect with others (not burden them) and take responsibility for it. This looks like a thoughtful, unpretentious discussion about the issue with even perhaps an openness to possible solutions.

Victimhood: In the short term, people can be victims of crimes directed at them. However, to see yourself as a victim in the long term, as the inevitable plaything of a world you did not create, misunderstood and alienated, is a helpless outlet for anxiety. Victimhood gets people to use their time and energy to feel sorry for you and fix your situation for you. It is not other peoples' responsibility to deal with your problem. Besides, the management of your anxiety is too important to hand over to others.

Criticism: It's easy to point out where other people mess up to make yourself feel better (it's fun too). This is why we have criticism—to distract ourselves from the pain of our own issue. Though not all criticism is created equal. There's constructive criticism, in which the purpose is to genuinely help who you criticize—you offer solutions, you're supportive. When you criticize as an effect of your perceived helplessness, you do it to hurt someone or to make yourself look or feel good by comparison.

Inability to take criticism: Often co-occurring with destructive criticism is the inability to take constructive criticism from others. Your criticism is often destructive, so you automatically interpret another's criticism as destructive, even when it's not.

Perfectionism: The purpose of perfectionism isn't our desire to be perfect—rather, it's our desire to beat ourselves up when we don't live up to our unattainable standards. To put it another way, we hold high standards for the purpose of feeling helpless. When the true motivations of perfectionism are revealed, it is better seen as a euphemism for masochism, which is also a sign of helplessness.

Martyrdom: This is one step beyond victimhood. When you use anxiety to be a victim, you get others to play into your illusion of persecution. With Martyrdom, you exaggerate your persecution specifically to elicit sympathy from others.

Passive-aggressiveness: This is when you indirectly inflict anxiety upon those who make you feel helpless in order to feel better about yourself. This is similar to martyrdom, but rather than elicit sympathy from others, you elicit sympathy from yourself.

Miscellaneous signs of helplessness: despair, toxic positivity, fatalism, feeling stuck, belief choices don't matter, an over-reliance on religion or God, an incessant self-admonishment to do what you "should" do, struggle addiction.

The portrait of helplessness
You wake up in the morning and immediately begin grumbling to yourself about what you need to do that day. *"Could life get any worse?"* you wonder. At work, your boss gives you more work than you can handle, and to deal with this you tell your coworkers about it at lunch. To get back at your boss, you hand the work back to him in a red folder as opposed to a manila folder, which you know isn't proper procedure, but it's not enough of a transgression for him to say anything.

After work you see a girl you want to talk to, but you wonder if there's any point to it. Women are damaged by whatever you perceive to be a degenerate culture, and besides they only like men who are tall, dark, and handsome.

When you get home you watch the news to submerse yourself in the horrors of the world. Suicide bombings, poverty, and starvation rationalize everything in your life that hasn't gone well or isn't going well.

You've been feeling helpless for years, and it's a drug your body craves. You need helplessness—no matter how horrible it makes you feel.

The way out of helplessness
If you're smart enough to read and understand this sentence, then you are never helpless. Helplessness is an illusion. There is always a solution to your situation, there is always something useful you can do with your anxiety. This brings us to the third and final way, and the only mature way, to handle anxiety.

3. Confrontation—the Constructive Way to Handle Anxiety

When you confront anxiety, you do not automatically turn away from it in avoidance. As you do with helplessness, you permit yourself to feel the anxiety. But the distinctive element of confrontation is when you feel the anxiety, you handle it in a mature way.

When we handle the anxiety in a mature way, the anxiety becomes a guide to action that benefits us as well as others in the environment. To do this, we think about our anxiety, what it could possibly indicate about our avoidance, and we consider others and what would benefit them.

The word "confrontation" may carry with it a negative connotation. But I use the word to express the mature way to handle anxiety because it's exactly what happens—you confront the anxiety for what it is, and so you confront reality for what it is, not how it appears through the lens of your anxiety. As there are many words for anxiety, there are many words for confrontation: "courage," "bravery," and "valor." If you're Spike Lee you can call it "do the right thing." Whatever works for you.

When you confront an anxious situation, you look down at the box of anxiety you hold and notice it makes your back sore. Instead of the regression to helplessness, you look for opportunity in the baggage. Maybe the situation seems dire, but you know now, because of the nature of anxiety, it is not. You can continue to lift the box until your back becomes stronger. Or you build a shelf in the garage for your box. Or you can find other people who carry around a similar box, and talk to them about it. In the process, you create friendships.

Maturity requires creativity. There is no one best way to handle anxiety maturely in every situation. Your confrontation depends on your values. (If your values are unknown or vague to you, confrontation may reveal your values to you. This is a process I clarify in Part III on *Identity*.) But as long as you can feel your anxiety and know, to your core, there is a mature solution to your anxiety, you're halfway home.

This is why it's crucial to see anxiety as an advantage—it is fuel you can use to make your life better. When you learn to use it in a mature way, anxiety can become, through the mechanism of your thought and your ability to make a decision, valuable for you and the world.

Confrontation is nothing more than a *decision* based on *thought*.

Let's look at the example of the electric bill. When you approach this situation with your newfound conception of anxiety, you neither throw the bill away in avoidance, nor do you lash out with impulsivity by grabbing a drink. You neither complain to your girlfriend about it, nor do you act like a victim and tell yourself the price-gouging electric company is out to get you, and there's no way poor little you could ever make it on his own in such a harsh world.

Rather, the stress of the anxiety compels you to take a step back and know, to your marrow, there is a solution. So you sit down for five minutes and decide if you simply cut down on beer for the next six weeks, you will save enough money to pay the bill. This helps the electric company because they get paid on time. This helps everyone in your life because now there's less of a chance of your regression to helpless behaviors. And this helps you because you may lose some weight now that your liver has more freedom to process other chemicals in your blood.

On a deeper level this also helps you because, when you manage the anxiety of the bill in a mature way, you implicitly tell yourself you're capable of managing anxiety well again in the future.

Another example of an anxiety-provoking situation is when we ask out a girl. The avoidance response is to not even think about asking her out. The anxiety may not even allow us to see her as a viable option. As we disconnect from ourselves and the anxiety we feel toward her, we disconnect from her.

The helpless response is to conclude there's nothing we can do about the situation anyway. We revert to criticism and complaints about girls. Girls necessarily become the enemy in our mind to justify the helplessness.

To confront the situation, we would need to talk to the girl in a way that is beneficial for her and for us. We are honest by treating her like the desired object she is, and we are respectful by treating her like the human she is. Perhaps we do not know how to strike this balance initially, so we may mess things up, but if we're willing to constantly learn, and not regress to helplessness or avoidance, we inevitably become more in tune with reality.

The worst-case scenario is she rejects us, but even if she does, she is pleased by our directness and decorum, and we leave her feeling better about herself.

This also leaves us better because we now actively confront fearful situations. In doing so, we confront the world as it is, not as it appears through the veil of anxiety. We gain something numinous when we use anxiety in a mature way—we gain confidence.

Confidence—the Prize of Confrontation

Anxiety is an energy, and when you use it for confrontation, you will, 100 percent of the time, sublimate the energy of that anxiety into the ability to confront anxiety in the future. The ability to confront anxiety is called confidence.

As men, we're constantly lectured about the importance of confidence. How a man's confidence is directly proportional to his satisfaction with life, his success with women, and the size of his bank account. Well, here you have the recipe for confidence, and it works every time.

Unlike the so-called confidence you may feel from a cool car and a lot of money, the confidence gained from confrontation is true, inner confidence. It's confidence that cannot be taken away. It is your resource. This will always be your prize for confrontation, and you will take it with you to your grave.

Confidence is transferable

A cool part about confidence is it's transferable.

Let's say you get an electric bill in the mail, and rather than avoid it you figure out a way to pay it through a beer reduction, as we discussed in the previous section. Since you handled the anxiety of the bill in a mature way, you feel more confidence. You can then use this confidence for the confrontation of other anxiety-provoking situations in your life.

When you're at work with your newfound confidence, you're more likely to communicate clearly to your boss, focus better on a problem, or you can use the confidence to form a work softball team. All this because you decided to confront your electric bill.

You will be more likely to confront situations you would have previously avoided, or situations that would have previously made you feel helpless. How much more likely? It depends on the amount of anxiety you're confronting. The more anxiety you confront, the more confidence you will gain.

This brings us to the **First Law of Confidence:**

The confidence we earn from confronting anxiety is directly proportional to the size of that anxiety.

Failure

Another cool part of confrontation is you don't need the right outcome to receive your confidence. You can fail, but as long as you did the courageous act, you will win the prize of confidence. This explains somebody who's an utter failure yet surprisingly confident. And they continue to get more confident even though they continue to fail. They're out in the world, consistently confronting their anxiety, and that's all that matters.

You don't need to be a success to be confident. Though the more confident you become, the more likely it is you will be successful. Consistent confrontation of reality in a productive way is the DNA of success.

For the broke and dateless who are confident, it's simply a matter of time before they're flush with money and women. They acquire something more important than success—they acquire the inner resource that will eventually lead to repeatable success.

This is where most men fail with anxiety. We all know, at least implicitly, we need to confront a fear in order to overcome that fear. But when we inevitably fail in our confrontation, we feel like our act of doing the right thing was in truth an act of doing the wrong thing. And we quit.

This brings us to the **Second Law of Confidence:**

Failure in an act of confrontation does not impede the accumulation of confidence.

One caveat of confrontation

You accumulate confidence when you recognize anxiety, then systematically face situations that are the source of your anxiety. However—and this is important—in order to transform your anxiety into confidence, you must confront your anxiety with 100 percent boldness. No peaking around the corner. No hemming. No hawing.

If we're afraid of speaking in public, for instance, we are allowed to fall on our face as we walk up to the podium, we are allowed to pee our pants, we are allowed to give our entire speech with our zipper down so everybody can see how tiny our penis is, which only confirms their assumption. But in the realm of confrontation, we are not allowed to half-ass it and say, "Sorry if I seem nervous, I don't speak in public often."

You're allowed to fail, and indeed failure will be necessary on your quest, but you must remain bold in that failure.

This is where the rest of men fail with anxiety. We must confront anxiety as if we've done it a thousand times before—otherwise the act will be empty.

Without boldness, you will not reap the full confidence of confrontation. You will confront anxiety, yet, for some reason, be unable to overcome the anxiety. At most, you'll feel relieved. This will implicitly convince you that you're stuck with the anxiety, that it's part of who you are, and you will give up.

This brings us to the **Third Law of Confidence:**

To gain confidence, we must be bold when we confront our anxiety.

Consistent action

One act of confrontation does transform your anxiety into confidence, but there is little hope that one act is sufficient for you to keep the confidence. It's possible, but unlikely.

For instance, if you ask out one girl, you will not be totally free of anxiety the next time you ask out a girl. You'll have less anxiety the second time, and you'll be more able to manage the anxiety, but anxiety will still be there.

However, one act of confrontation may change even your character if it is, at least in your eyes, courageous enough. Let's say a young boy stands up to his mom's boyfriend who abuses both him and her. This one act of confrontation may have a drastic impact on his confidence for years to come, if not the rest of his life. Through the challenge of a larger, older, abusive male at a young age, the boy may change his self-concept.

Most acts of confrontation don't have this impact on us. To get over most fears, it takes about 30 days of consistent confrontation to remove the anxiety. This is at least what the research says, but in my experience, it takes more like 90 days, and quite honestly, it could take years. This depends on you, your personality, genetic factors, and past trauma.

But give yourself at least 30 days to confront the anxiety every day, then take a step back and see how you feel. If the anxiety is still there, then keep at it and know you're on the right track.

Exposure Therapy

When a flat-out confrontation of your anxiety feels like too much to take on at once, you need to ramp yourself up to do it. This is called exposure therapy, and there are five levels to it.

1. Acquire knowledge. Let's say you want to ask for a raise at work, but merely the thought of asking for a raise gives you a panic attack. Your first act of confrontation, therefore, would be to acquire knowledge about the anxious situation. In this case, you could create a list of reasons why you deserve a raise. If you ask for a raise with legitimate reasons, this will make the confrontation much easier. Most anxiety, however, doesn't stem from lack of knowledge. Otherwise, nerds would be confident.

2. Visualization. Build a picture in your mind of what it would be like to ask for a raise. Imagine how it would feel, how your boss would react, and how you would ask. With visualization, every detail counts, because every detail contributes to your emotional state. You may need to write out the scenario to make it more real for you.

Use role play the help with the visualization. Get a friend to play the part of your boss and have him respond in a reasonable way to your confrontation. Even have your friend play up the part and act as a comical, robber baron stereotype. This will seem funny to you, as it is. You will often laugh as you confront anxiety. We laugh when we begin to see something larger than the pettiness of the apparent. How would you make an eagle funny? You would make him afraid of mice.

3. Observation. Watch somebody else do what you're afraid to do. For this example, there are videos online that show someone asking for a raise. As you watch, you'll feel what it would be like to ask for a raise, which will acclimate your nervous system that much more.

4. Desensitization. Confront a similar threat, but one that's less anxiety-provoking. If you're too afraid to ask your boss for a raise, ask for a discount on an item from the hardware store. Hey, you've been going there for years, they owe you.

5. Exposure. Finally, you're ready for the full confrontation, or at least as ready as you're going to be.

I recommend exposure therapy for anxiety because it can work well. But be wary of it because we can easily get stuck at any of these steps, especially step one and step four. Even for a particularly big confrontation, spend no more than one week on each step, so the entire process will take about a month. A month is still long in my opinion, but if one situation causes you that much anxiety, then so be it.

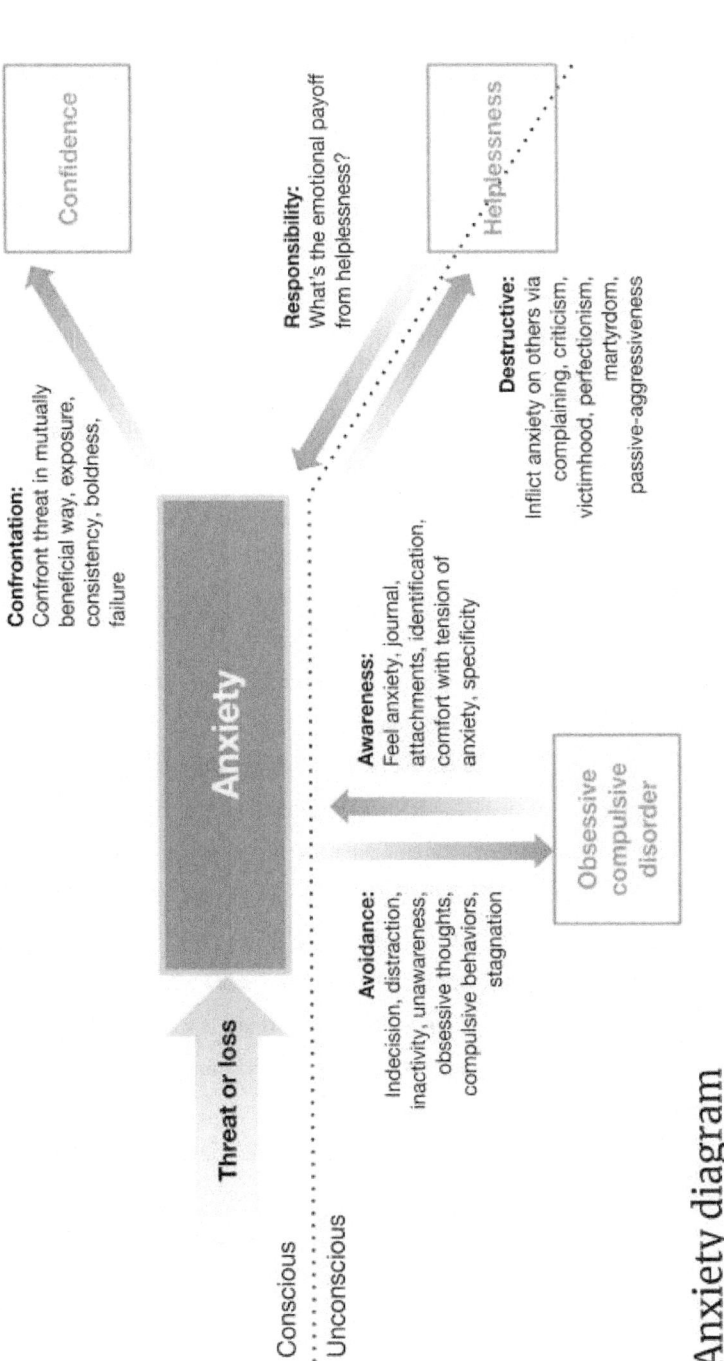

Anxiety diagram

Threat or loss → Anxiety

Conscious / Unconscious

Confrontation: Confront threat in mutually beneficial way, exposure, consistency, boldness, failure → **Confidence**

Responsibility: What's the emotional payoff from helplessness?

Destructive: Inflict anxiety on others via complaining, criticism, victimhood, perfectionism, martyrdom, passive-aggressiveness → **Helplessness**

Awareness: Feel anxiety, journal, attachments, identification, comfort with tension of anxiety, specificity

Avoidance: Indecision, distraction, inactivity, unawareness, obsessive thoughts, compulsive behaviors, stagnation → **Obsessive compulsive disorder**

Excitement: The Mastery of Anxiety

In the beginning of this part of the book, I mentioned there are different words for anxiety, like worry, concern, and dread. Well, there's another word for anxiety: excitement. Excitement is anxiety you know how to handle—it is anxiety comforted by a bed of confidence.

Physiologically, we cannot tell the difference between excitement and anxiety. If we looked at the functional images of the brains of two people, one who feels anxiety and the other who feels excitement, they would look similar. The only difference is how well each person is acclimated to his emotional state.

As you learn how to manage your anxiety, you will begin to view it as excitement. Of course you will—you anticipate the good your anxiety brings to your life. Anxiety becomes the pathway to growth.

Anxiety feels like excitement when you internalize threats as pathways to growth.

This is the endgame of anxiety—to feel the anxiety you always felt, but now it feels like excitement. Since you now confront the excitement, it flows into confidence. Your old thoughts of "I can't, but I have to" become "I could if I want, but I won't if I choose not to."

Complaints become affirmation, victimhood becomes responsibility, and passive-aggressiveness becomes communication.

New challenges cause new excitement, which naturally flows into more confidence.

When you exercise your ability to properly feel and process anxiety, you create a perpetual source of nutrition for your psychology.

Conclusion: The Anxiety Never Ends
An act of confrontation transforms anxiety into confidence, but this is only the beginning. As you clear out the anxiety in one area of your psyche, this allows you to see the anxiety in other areas of your psyche. It's like clearing out a crawl space. All you can see is the first layer of junk, and when you clear out that first layer, it reveals to you the next layer you couldn't see before. Then the next. Then the next.

This removal of the anxious accumulation isn't an endless struggle, though. As you continue to clear out your anxiety, you begin to see the world differently. You realize you only saw the world a certain way because of how it appeared to you through the veil of anxiety.

What once looked like doubt now looks like opportunity. What once looked like worry now looks like fun. You'll also begin to see yourself differently, and for the same reason—you only saw yourself as you appeared through the veil of anxiety.

The anxiety becomes a fun challenge you can manage. As such, the world becomes a fun challenge you can manage. As the anxiety begins to make sense, the world begins to make sense, and you'll make sense to the world.

Your decisions and perceptions will be true, and you will be meant to live on this earth.

Part II: Anger

How to become compassionate by understanding your anger.

The noble man accepts the fact of anger without a question mark;
He knows anger guides the soul, that it is for the few,
the privilege of the strong.
He has rechristened the evil as good, thus his life is owed to the evil.
– Friedrich Nietzsche

What Anger Is

Anger is a signal from your environment that tells you to achieve something. There is something, either existentially or psychologically, that is at least a perceivable need to you, and anger is your body's adaptation to let you know this. The need could be concrete—like a job, girlfriend, or bigger apartment. Or it could be abstract—like the need to be understood, or the need to be comfortable with who you are.

Another way to view anger is as the injustice emotion—an unmet need can also be viewed as an injustice. Something is wrong, according to your values, so you *need* to make it right.

There are other words for anger: "Annoyed," "bored," "vengeful," "frustrated," "pissed off," "enraged," or "troubled." But these words merely describe various shades of anger. We use language to tease apart the intricacies of our psychological states, but ultimately, it's all anger. And all anger, no matter how you describe it, and no matter the degree to which you feel it, is managed in fundamentally the same way.

Though anger is often seen as a negative experience, this is only our perception of it. In truth, there is nothing wrong with anger, and it can even be one of our greatest gifts when we understand how to use it. But first, it's essential to see anger as nothing more than a signal from your environment that tells you to achieve something.

The Purpose of *Part II: Anger*

The purpose of *Part II: Anger* isn't to completely free your life of anger. Anger is a natural part of life, and it will keep coming up for you in different forms. It will be triggered by different instances throughout your life, and that's healthy.

If you never feel any anger, then that means you're content with less than you deserve, or you're unaware of the anger.

Rather than eliminate anger, the purpose of this part of the book is to help you master your anger. This means the ability to turn your anger into something useful. When you apply the information in this book, eventually you will get to the point where you see anger as a good thing because you will be in control of it instead of it controlling you. Your feeling of anger will become a herald of growth.

Mastering your anger can be difficult, like climbing a mountain. Fortunately, it's also simple, like climbing a mountain—keep putting one foot in front of the other and you'll get there. After all, there are only two causes of anger, and only three ways to handle anger.

Let's begin with the two causes of anger.

The Two Causes of Anger
In no particular order:
    1. An unmet need
    2. An injustice
That's it, the only two causes of anger.

An injustice is a need that is taken away from you.

And an unmet need is, well, something you need but do not have.

You could effectively equate "an unmet need" with "injustice," but I distinguish between the two for clarification.

You could think of your need to make $100,000 per year in comparison with your current salary of $75,000 as an injustice. And you could think of the injustice of a false accusation as a need to communicate the truth.

Another way to view an unmet need and an injustice is as a hurt, or a harm.

When you experience an injustice, you are harmed. When you have a need taken away, you are hurt. Anger is your body's mechanism to alert you of the harm, and it's your fuel to alleviate the harm.

Part II: Anger

Let's say you've worked at a law firm for the last 12 years, and you're on track to make partner. Your father made partner by the time he was 37, and so will you. You work ever hour and rub every elbow.

One day, the head of the firm calls you into his office. "This is it," you think. "Everything is according to plan."

However, he doesn't make you partner—he fires you.

A need has gone unmet, an injustice has occurred. You become angry.

You may yell and fight and scream. You may feel like you've been lied to. You may feel like you've been led on. You may feel, deep down, that because you didn't get the partnership, you're not the man you thought you were—you're at least not the man your father was. That hurts.

You will most likely feel anxiety because of this. You will worry. Where can I find a job now? What will everybody think? But the prevalent emotion here will most likely be anger because you expected the situation to turn out otherwise. You felt an injustice was inflicted upon you.

The injustice in this situation will most likely be overwhelming, in which case you won't know how to handle the anger. Your psychology will be like a bone that cracks under too much pressure.

This brings us to the first decision you can make with anger.

1. Sadness—the Self-Destructive Way to Handle Anger

When anger feels too great to handle, you will collapse under the weight of it. The injustice is too huge or the need is too unattainable, so there's nothing you could do about it no matter what you thought or did. As a result, you will be unable to make a decision about what to do with the anger. Sadness, to put it another way, is anger stored up. It is anger you do nothing with. But even no decision is still a decision.

We have a difficult time making the connection between sadness and anger at first, so the next time you're sad, make a list of what you need, and you will begin to get angry. As you become aware of sadness and what causes it, the sadness will turn into anger.

Therefore, sadness can be thought of as the third "cause" of anger. I put "cause" in quotations because, technically, sadness doesn't cause anger. Sadness *is* anger.

When you become aware of your sadness, it will make you angry. You get in touch with the unmet needs, or injustices, that caused the anger in the first place.

We also feel sad in response to anger when we view anger as a negative state. It's a common belief that anger, or animus, ahem, is a bad thing. But as we have already learned, it is not a bad thing. It is a tool, like a gun. You can use the gun to defend yourself and kill a deer to feed your family, or you could use that gun to rob a liquor store.

**Your anger is always justified—
what you do with your anger is not.**

We may feel that anger is an inherent vice because it makes us feel powerful. Anger is, after all, a stimulant—and I do mean it is literally a stimulant. An angry mind is similar to a mind pumped full of stimulants. It's energic yet easy to focus. Anger, like stimulants, causes a rise in dopamine levels in the brain, flushes the skin, and increases the heart rate. This is our body's adaptation so we can do what we need to do to get what we need. The release of these chemicals is our brain's way to prepare an action.

When we shut down our anger, we're still angry. We only made ourselves unaware of the anger because we're afraid to stand out and be noticed. A man who has done anything of significance is a man who is in touch with his anger and uses it to get what he needs. These men understand, perhaps unconsciously, that anger is nothing more than an emotional signal that tells them to achieve something.

The good in sadness

As we can understand anger as healthy, it's important to realize sadness is healthy as well. Like anger, sadness is only as good as its context.

If we experience a devastating event, like a job termination when we expected a job promotion, it's normal to feel sad. It's normal to feel besieged by the incident. It's normal to turn frustration in on ourselves. There's overwhelming evidence that sadness, in certain amounts, helps us cope with injustices. It helps us begin to formulate a strategy for the attainment of needs. Men who are sad have been shown to make better decisions, develop a healthier perspective, and set healthier expectations (ie boundary, which we'll discuss in the next part on identity).

When you feel sad, you are more likely to figure out your needs.

Sadness, when handled properly, carries with it the seed of its own destruction.

Sadness is not only a part of who we are; it probably even *made* us who we are. It's an important tool that keeps us connected in difficult times. Men who look out for each other are more able to work together. Men who work together survive.

This is all a way to say sadness is okay. Recognize it's in you to be sad as a result of an injustice. Give yourself time to let yourself be sad. This is your designated sad time. Sit with the sadness. Understand the sadness is not only temporary, but healthy.

When we never experience sadness, this is always a much more serious problem than the sadness itself.

But sadness is only productive to a point. As it is in our nature to increase group cohesion over sadness, it would be disadvantageous to always be sad. Humans would never get anything done because we had too many group hugs on our schedule.

Sadness is constructive in the short-term,
but destructive in the long-term.

After six months of perpetual sadness, it is no longer sadness and it becomes depression. There's a six-month limit on sadness because around this time, the sadness begins to influence your brain chemistry. In a sense, your brain acclimates to sadness, so it takes on a saddened state as given. This, inevitably, puts a lot of stress on the body.

So it takes six months for sadness to become a disorder, but research indicates it's healthiest to manage sadness in two weeks to one month. Men who spend this amount of time with the sadness recover better from the harm, and they even have fond memories of the harm. They do more than recover—they become stronger.

A story from my life
Over the past several months, I have been growing increasingly unsettled. Something wasn't right, and that something had grown larger and larger in my psyche. Then, a few days ago, it hit me. I was watching the original Cosmos series (episode eight) and I

Part II: Anger

felt a deep deficiency, like I was unable to live up to a certain, requisite standard. The sadness came, and it came hard. It felt like my brain completely shut down. But it was only in this state of sadness that I was able to truly feel one of my unmet needs: my work. Specifically, I felt the need to make my work, which includes this book, as helpful as possible, though for the past several months I have been in slack-off mode. Thousands of young men are going to read this (hopefully), and if it's no good, then I have done them a great disservice. Moreover, I'm going to read this, and if it's no good, then I have done myself a great disservice.

The thought of this need was in the back of my mind for a while, but it took the overwhelming burden of sadness—triggered by the thought of myself as sentient starstuff—for me to get in touch with it. Only then was I able to fall asleep and wake up the next day, more committed than ever.

It took the sadness to get in touch with my disowned need. It felt horrible in the short-term, but in the long-term, I was invigorated.

Sadness is a drill that tunnels ever deeper into your psyche to find out what's beneath your range of perception.

I want you to feel sad. I want your sadness to keep your head on the pillow for an entire day. I want you to become so overwhelmed with sadness you break down and cry—just not in front of anyone else. And never admit when you do, because yeah, that would be lame.

The way out of sadness

When it is time to emerge from your sadness, you must first learn how to feel your anger. Understand anger, and all the powerful hues that come with it, is a good and noble state. Your anger doesn't make you bad, it makes you magnanimous.

The other half of the battle is to become more comfortable with the anger and so feel it. You most likely have become an expert at shutting it down before you can feel it, so your body has had little chance to acclimate to those anger chemicals.

In this respect, anger is no different than a 300-pound squat. You're able to squat a 300-pound barbell right now. Unless you have muscular dystrophy, you have enough muscle in your legs to squat 300 pounds. But why can't you? Your neurological system cannot handle it. You haven't trained your brain to work in conjunction with the muscles in your legs to squat that much weight. On your quest for a 300-pound squat, you will probably put on some muscle, but you'll mostly be able to squat the 300 pounds because you train your nervous system to handle the tension of the weight.

I remember a couple years ago when I added about 20 percent to my squat. The size of my thighs barely increased. Rather, I increased the load my neuromuscular system could handle.

To feel your anger is no different. It is a neurological load. This is demonstrated in men who don't let themselves feel angry often. When these men do get angry, they begin to shake uncontrollably from the tension. Same thing happens when you squat a lot of weight.

This is a truth bouncers understand well when a fight breaks out in a bar. They know to be more wary of the guy who has a steely stare than the guy who flies off the handle at the slightest provocation. The guy whose pulse stays under 80 when a fight occurs has become comfortable with the tension of a fight. In other words, he's been there before.

But you cannot feel your anger unless you first learn what causes your sadness. The simplest way to do this, as I have mentioned, is to make a list of your needs.

**To go from sadness to anger,
all you need is time and self-awareness.**

Here are a few questions to get your journal started:

What could be causing your anger?
Why do you keep yourself from getting angry?
What would you think of yourself if you got angry?
In what ways do you fear your anger?
What do you feel when you see other men getting angry?
What do you need? (this one's my favorite—simple, powerful)

These are also helpful questions to answer with a therapist. A therapist will not help you manage your anger. Only you can do that. But if a therapist is good for one thing, it's to be a well-educated and experienced mirror that reflects back to you what you are. (But don't talk about your therapy too much. There is no shame in therapy, but to prattle on about it is shameful.)

Once you learn to feel your anger and what specifically makes you angry, you can still do something immature with it. This brings us to the second way to handle anger.

2. Hostility—the Destructive Way to Handle Anger

When we act in a hostile way, we feel the anger rather than let it fester into sadness, which is good. But we use it to hurt others instead. We make others manage our anger through hostility. The hurt and injustice we feel is the same hurt and injustice we inflict upon others. Hostility can be done consciously, but when we hold on to a lot of anger, and we do not know how to handle it properly, it will inevitably be done unconsciously.

Men act hostile because they see themselves as powerless to manage the anger on their own, so they must inflict others with it as their only way of relief.

There are other words for hostility, most notably "aggression." But "aggression" is too often used to pathologize healthy behavior, which I will discuss in the next section. Plus, I use "hostility" because it is the proper psychological term for what we describe here (pinkies up!).

Both the cause and effect of hostility is a mindset that views the world as a place in which others must lose in order for you to win. This is colloquially referred to as having a scarcity mentality. Economically, it's a zero-sum mentality. By way of this deficient thought model, resources and wealth are viewed as limited, so in order for one man to win, another man must lose.

To the scarcity mindset, there is only so much money, there is only so much luxury, there is only so much food, and there is only so much friendship and love.

But anything you could ever want that would heal harm or rectify an injustice or achieve a need is nothing more than a value. And all value you see around you, whether it's a house or a car or a lifestyle, is created, first and foremost, by a decision based on thought.

**Decisions and thought are infinite;
to see the world as a scarce place is a fallacy.**

When a man designs a bridge, it's a decision he makes based on his knowledge of engineering.

When a man writes a book, it's a decision he makes based on his knowledge of the subject of the book.

When a man attends graduate school to become a psychologist, it's a decision he makes based on his knowledge that he's a dork.

None of these men borrow, or steal, or take from any other man to do what they want. To quote the humungous Terry Crews, "There is no pie you need to get a piece of—the whole world is a kitchen."

And to quote the not-as-humungous me, "If humans were lions, we'd build antelope factories, and lions from different prides would work together to make more antelope than they could ever eat."

When a man acts with hostility through a scarcity mindset, he lacks the thought it takes to get his needs met on his own. And he lacks the decision it takes to implement that thought on his own.

Though we all act hostile at times, so we need to be aware of it when we do. Awareness of our destructive thoughts and behaviors is necessary to put a stop to them. Here are the most common forms of hostility:

Jealousy: When another man achieves something, this increases your ability to achieve that thing. Value begets value. But if you view the success of another man through a scarcity mindset, his success necessarily impedes your success. Hence, jealously.

Preemptive violence: When you hurt others preemptively, you hurt them in the same way you hurt. Not to dissuade you from violence, because violence is fun. So think of it this way: fights are good, attacks are bad. Even a bar fight can be healthy when done in the gentlemanly conduct of trading punches. I may even go as far to say being physically overpowered, even humiliated, by another man is part of a healthy initiation.

Revenge: This is when we direct hostility to hurt someone who caused an injustice or harm we felt in the past. True, revenge can be justified when done in a *The Count of Monte Cristo*, righting-a-cosmic-wrong, kind of way. But be careful with this because while Edmond Dantes used revenge for good at first, it eventually overtook his life, which I'm sure is at least part of the point of that story.

Resentment: Technically, resentment isn't hostility, but it may cause hostility. Resentment is when we feel anger but do nothing with it. Yet we remain focused on it in perpetuity, so it doesn't collapse into sadness. Resentment causes hostility because it's impossible to hold on to anger too long before it slips through your fingers. When men are resentful, they often become attached to it. Resentment is the basis for grudges.

Verbal abuse: The implication of verbal abuse is you must make others feel bad in order to make yourself feel good. This comes up for most men in their interactions with women. When a woman says something mean, men feel like they need to come over the top with a zingy rejoinder. Let her hostility be her hostility, and turn away in a "Whelp, have a good life" kind of way.

Temper tantrums: This may come as a surprise to my New Jersey readers, but temper tantrums don't make you more of a man. They only make you look like a man in front of other guys who also mistakenly think temper tantrums are manly. It's a way to get attention, and attention assuages the discomfort that comes from your inability to deal with your anger properly.

Theft: When we steal, it says "There is no way I could have earned this on my own. After all, achievement is difficult."

Hostility begets hostility: Another sign of hostility is when other men act hostile toward us on a consistent basis. This is the nature of hostility. When we act hostile toward others, they act hostile toward us. It only seems like others are out to get us because we're out to get them. About one in ten guys are jackasses and it's their problem. But when it seems like five in ten are jackasses, then it's our problem.

A story from my life

I used to have a roommate who was messier than I was. When he would leave his dishes out, or failed to unclog the drain in the shower, I would all but attack him to clean up. My request came from a place of "I cannot believe this guy is such an idiot," which he felt. Then when he would act like a jerk to me, I would think he was the problem. Later, I was shocked to learn I may have been the problem.

Miscellaneous signs of hostility: exclusion of others, gossip, the purposeful disregard of someone, ad hominem, the spread of rumors, erroneous blame.

In essence, hostility is when we need to hurt someone else in order to heal our own sense of hurt. Of course, hostility doesn't heal us—it only seems like that because it's a distraction from our anger. When we hurt others to get what we want, nobody will be more hurt by the hostility than we will be.

If we steal a man's car, for instance, he's only out a car. In the big picture, that's no big deal. As long as his mind isn't infected with scarcity, he can make money and buy another car. But when we steal his car, we teach ourselves the only way to get by in the world is through the hurt of others. This will pay dividends in self-destructive decisions for years to come.

This won't merely influence how we see cars, of course. This will influence how we relate with men in all areas of life. How do we get money? Bilk others. How do we feel big? Make others feel small. We need to get ours before other men get theirs.

Let's go back to the example of the lawyer who was fired. If he became hostile as a result of being fired, he would inflict his anger onto others to make them feel a similar sort of hurt he feels. He would key his boss's car. He would steal from the company on his last day. He would be verbally abusive to his boss or whoever else he felt wronged him while he was at the firm. He would spread gossip about whoever was named partner instead of him.

This may make him feel good, or not bad, in the short term, but ultimately, his anger is still with him, and it's still his and his alone to handle. He has not advanced his situation. Even worse, through hostility he teaches himself he must hurt others order to feel good about himself, which doesn't last long anyway. It's always a Pyrrhic victory. Though we convince ourselves distraction feels good if that's all we have. When we carry this premise to its logical conclusions, it won't be long until we're lonely and broke.

A story from my life

When I was in college, I wrote for the alternative newspaper on campus. My articles were better than the articles at the main paper. This, at least, was the story I told myself. Yet my supposed genius went unrecognized. I felt angry because of this—it felt like an injustice. So I would terrorize campus with my debauchery. There was many an upper deck left in a sorry state. I felt entitled because, after all, I was a genius who nobody was smart enough to recognize (in my mind).

The way out of hostility

If you are smart enough to read and understand this sentence, then there is never a reason for hostility. Chimpanzees must be hostile. They have little intelligence and no imagination from which to create value from sentient decisions. But even if you're from New Jersey, you are far more intelligent than a chimp. You do have a choice.

This brings us to the third and final decision, and only mature decision, to make with anger.

3. Assertiveness—the Constructive Way to Handle Anger

When we use anger to make a constructive decision, we neither let it build up in sadness, nor do we hurt others with it. Instead, we look at the anger for what it is, listen for what it tells us to get, and think of a way to get it while we help others get what they want. This is the nature of assertiveness.

I use the word "assertiveness" to denote the constructive way to handle anger because it entails a placement forth, or assertion, of our needs to the world. Through assertiveness, we express the sentiment, "Here is what I want, and here is a way I can create what I want. And ultimately, this doesn't ask a lot because we live in a world conducive to what we want."

As I implied earlier, "aggression" is often used to pathologize healthy, assertive behavior when the assertive behavior is conspicuous and extreme. But as long as you are assertive in the strict sense of what assertiveness means—to create value for others as well as yourself—then there's no such thing as too much assertiveness. Too much assertiveness is like too much charm. It's like too much money. It's like too many Shake Shack burgers. It's like too many pertinent examples.

When you work with the material in this book and understand your anger for what it is, weaker men will accuse you of aggressiveness when you are unapologetically assertive. Accept this as part of your role as someone who gains status, and smile and nod.

The denouncement of assertiveness reminds me of a story of a teenager who developed a new app and wanted TechCrunch to cover it. He proceeded to email the TechCrunch writers more than a thousand times. When this was reported, everyone criticized this kid for being too aggressive. They called him other pejoratives like "entitled," "snotty," "bratty." But in truth the kid offered a win-win proposition to TechCrunch—the kid would get his need to be publicized met, and TechCrunch would get their need to have a provocative story met (well, you know, provocative for the tech industry). Eventually, TechCrunch did write a story about the app.

Part II: Anger

Aggression wins.

When you understand assertiveness as a creation of value, this makes it much easier to be as "aggressive" as you want. When you know you offer value to others, it's natural to be relentless. Imagine if someone paid you 100 dollars to give one million dollars to a children's hospital, but for whatever reason, the hospital didn't accept the money. You wouldn't stop after one "no." You wouldn't stop after 100 "no's." It's also natural to be relentless when you understand any criticism hurled your way will be unfounded.

Let's look at assertiveness through the example of the fired lawyer. Once you get fired, you may become sad if the injustice and hurt of the situation is too much to manage at first. You may be unable for a bit to make decisions about what you need. As we stated, this is often a healthy and natural response to an injustice, and we may need time to decompress.

After two to four weeks, because you journal and introspect, you will begin to feel the anger and tune into what the anger tells you to do about the injustice.

At first, your anger may direct you toward hostility, so you will want to take a baseball bat to stolen office property and recreate other iconic scenes from *Office Space*. But you're able to read this book, so you would rather look at the anger for what it is and then assert it.

What specifically could you need when you're fired instead of promoted? You need another job. You need money. You need to feel like you contribute to society.

On a deeper level, you may need to know why you were fired. Awareness of a hurtful situation is often a necessary component of assertiveness.

It's easy to imagine how being fired would make us angry. But it's just as easy to imagine if we had all those needs met, then we would be much less likely to become sad or act out in hostility. If we had those needs met, then whether we were fired would matter much less.

Perhaps because he was fired, the lawyer learns he was only a lawyer because his dad was a lawyer, and he had only lived in his shadow his entire life. He didn't need that promotion. In truth, he needed to be his own man, and it took a job terminus to realize this.

With the use of thought and decision, you can see how any injustice you may experience can become a value.

Everybody wins, and all it took from you was to understand anger as a signal from your environment that tells you to achieve something.

A story from my life
Recently I was at the library and there was a guy and a girl at the table next to me. They were talking a little bit too loudly for a library. I wanted to curse them out because seriously, what kind of deranged maniac talks at the library?

But, because I know anger is a signal to get my needs met while I help others get their needs met, I placed the anger out in the world in a nice way as I suggested they get a private study room, which is available on the ninth floor. It turns out they had never been to this library before, so they didn't know about the private study rooms on the ninth floor. They both apologized and thanked me and were on their way. Their life is better; my life is better.

Through the use of anger as fuel for action to attain what we need, we achieve something much more important than what we originally needed.

Compassion—the Prize of Assertiveness
When we use our anger to assert our needs and get them met in a constructive way, we will feel compassion.

Compassion is the ability to see the world as a place in which men can achieve their needs through production.

Compassion takes on many forms. It can be demonstrated as charity, kindness, and general beneficence. This depends on the type of man you are. For instance, some men express compassion through gifts. While others, no matter how compassionate they are, do not like to give gifts. Rather, they would sooner spend time with someone or help them by, say, giving them a ride to the airport.

Unfortunately, compassion has become synonymous with softness and femininity. This connotation is unfounded. The essence of compassion is creativity. Without the ability to be creative, we see our needs and the needs of others as a burden.

Through creativity, our needs and the needs of others are a challenge to grow. There's nothing soft about it.

In *Part I: Anxiety*, we learned confidence, the prize of a confrontation with anxiety, is the sense you are capable. Compassion is the sense the world is conducive to capability. Confidence and compassion complement each other. When you are both confident and compassionate, you live in a world conducive to your desires, and you are capable to achieve your desires.

It makes sense, therefore, when you become more able to get your needs met, you become more compassionate.

As compassion is the prize of the proper management of sadness and hostility, it is the antidote to sadness and hostility. A man who has high levels of compassion will still become angry. He has needs, he will be hurt, and injustices will forever abound. But every time he turns his anger into compassion, he will become that much more likely to turn future anger into compassion.

Compassion is the antidote to anger and the value gained from its sublimation. You have within you the psychological muscle to do this—you only need to make it stronger.

False compassion

Make no mistake—assertiveness is the only way to be compassionate. Compassion is a worldview; a message you speak to yourself. You cannot pretend to be compassionate any more than you can pretend to be a Jew if you're Muslim. You may be able to fake compassion for a while, but other men will see through your smarminess. Even worse, it becomes more difficult to handle anger maturely when we pretend it's not there.

When you feel true compassion, you genuinely express it to others because you see the world as a benevolent place in which there is enough to go around for everybody.

> *A story from my life*
> *I have a friend who makes a lot of money. He confides in me that he needs to tell me about his successes because he cannot tell anyone else. "You're the only one who seems genuinely happy for me. Everyone else seems jealous. They pretend to be happy for me but you can tell they're fake." Of course I wouldn't be fake. The more for him, the more for me, the more for everybody. Wow, I'm such a great guy.*

When you employ assertiveness to get your injustices rectified and your needs met, you feel all the bountiful compassion that results from it. This feels fantastic. An injustice or hurt that once seemed like the most horrible moment in your life has become one of the greatest, all because of the capacity for thought and decision within you. Again, this feels fantastic.

This is always how it works with compassion. The more compassion you have from assertiveness, the more compassion you will have for beneficence. The only way to truly help someone is to do it through compassion, and the only way to have compassion is to master your anger.

One caveat of compassion

When we assert anger, a failure to get needs met doesn't transform the anger into compassion. Anger doesn't care about good intentions. Failure only makes us more angry, which of course can be a good thing. The more we fail, the more we get in touch with our unmet needs. And the more anger we feel, the more energy we have to get needs met. But we do not master the anger and achieve compassion until we successfully get our needs met.

We must achieve what it is we need in order to earn compassion.
To master anger, we must be successful.

Good thing we live in a world conducive to success.

Anger diagram

Conscious

Unconscious

Need or injustice → **Anger**

Avoidance: Discomfort with anger, distraction, numb senses, inactivity, unawareness, indecision, stagnation → Sadness/depression

Awareness: List needs, list injustices, list what you want, be specific about what you want, become comfortable with tension of anger

Assertiveness: Get needs met and injustices rectified in a way that is mutually beneficial → Compassion

Responsibility: What's the emotional payoff from hostility?

Destructive: Inflict anger on others to get your needs met and rectify injustices → Hostility

Desire—the Mastery of Anger

In the beginning of this book, I mentioned there are different words for anger, like annoyed, frustrated, enraged, and upset. Well, there's another word for anger: desire. Desire is anger you know how to handle—it is anger comforted by compassion.

Physiologically, we cannot tell the difference between desire and anger. If you looked at the functional images of the brains of two men, one who feels anger and the other who feels desire, the images would look similar. The only difference is how well each man is acclimated to his emotional state.

As you learn how to manage your anger, you will begin to view it as desire. You will be an angry man, but nobody would ever think of you as an angry man. Instead of the regression to hostility or sadness, you listen to what your anger tells you to get. Then you use this thought with a decision to achieve what you need. As you master this process, anger begins to feel like desire as you anticipate the good your needs and injustices bring to your life.

Anger feels like desire when you internalize your needs as pathways to growth.

This is the endgame of anger—you feel the anger you always felt, but now you identify it as desire. Since you assert the desire, it flows into compassion. Your old sadness comes to the surface as desire, and you handle it as such. As you trust yourself to feel more and more anger, the desire becomes stronger and stronger.

Resentment becomes communication, violence becomes negotiation, and destruction becomes construction.

New needs and injustices cause new desire, which naturally flows into new compassion.

When you properly feel and process anger, you create a perpetual source of nutrition for your psychology.

Conclusion—Grief and Happiness

Though anger and anxiety are separate emotions, they often both appear together. Anxiety and anger are like light and heat—you study them separately though it's rare to find one without the other.

It makes sense. A loss that causes anxiety could also be an injustice. And it is often necessary for you to confront your anxiety in order to assert your anger.

Anger and anxiety can also exist in equal amounts. When we feel a significant amount of anger and anxiety in equal amounts and at the same time, this is grief.

The combination of anger and anxiety is grief.

Previously on my podcast, I discussed how grief is a pathway to self-awareness and emotional mastery. Now you know why. Where there is grief, there is anxiety and anger—where there is anxiety and anger, there is your fear and your need. Where there is fear and need, there is all the information about yourself, the world, and what is required of you to engage more with it.

Conversely, happiness occurs when you've learned to master your anger and anxiety. When you do this, you have met your needs (asserted anger), and you are secure with your needs (confronted anxiety). You are compassionate and confident.

The combination of compassion and confidence is happiness.

I've received criticism over my deconstruction of emotions because I only focus on the "negative" emotions of anger and anxiety. Except anger and anxiety are not negative emotions. They may feel negative when they're misunderstood or avoided, but that doesn't make them so. A classic novel like *War and Peace* may feel like a bore—ie negative—when you don't understand it, but when you do understand it, you see it as full of information and a fun challenge.

Your anger and anxiety are like *War and Peace*, but greater. As Hugo says, "To write a poem of the human consciousness would be to swallow up all epics in a superior and definite epic."

Neither are anger nor anxiety positive emotions—they are *pathways* to positive emotions. Anger and anxiety are lenses into your own psyche that tell you what you must do. Positive emotions tell you nothing about what you must do—they only tell you what you have done.

A book on happiness or self-esteem would be like a book on marathon preparation that only discussed how to enjoy yourself after you win. The only sentence that ever needs to be written about happiness is this: Enjoy it and share it as much as possible when you learn how to manage anger and anxiety.

Now that you have the tools for emotional mastery, enjoy your life and share it as much as possible.

Part III: Identity

How to become strong by understanding your weakness.

"To put it practically is to put it theoretically: Your identity is who you are… who you are as a man of the species and as an individual. It is either the most complex of subjects, or it is the most simple of subjects, depending on how well you see yourself."

– Carl Jung

What Identity Is

To channel Carl Jung, identity is what we are as a man of the species and as an individual. It is composed of three parts:
1. Mind,
2. Decisions, and
3. The psychological boundary, which is how our mind and decisions combine to impact the world.

So this part is divided into three chapters. First, I will discuss the mind and how it affects decisions. Then I will discuss decisions and how they affect the mind. Then I will discuss the boundary, and how it is created by our decisions and our mind.

This process happens thousands of times per day, regardless of whether we're aware of it. It is the process by which we become who we are. This occurs even if we do not make a decision, and it occurs even if we do not understand what our mind is. It happens whether we've studied psychology our entire life, and it happens if we've never given the subject a thought.

This process creates our values, which mediate and moderate anger and anxiety. This process is what we use to choose our friends, choose a career, and choose our life. And it's what we don't use when we let others choose these things for us.

As you have created your identity, it has created you—and your world. Look around you right now. Your identity is reflected in your surroundings and circumstances. Everything you think and feel, everything you say and do, everything that is you.

Your identity is your personality. It is your character. It is your Self. It is your God.

It's that important, so let's learn about it.

The Purpose of *Part III: Identity*

As confrontation makes you confident, and as assertiveness makes you compassionate, your identity makes you strong—psychologically strong.

The purpose of *Part III: Identity* isn't to completely free your life of weakness. Weakness is a natural part of life, and it will arise for you in different forms.

If you never feel weak, then that means you never challenge yourself to learn and grow, or you're unaware of your weakness.

Instead, the purpose of *Identity* is to help you master your weakness. This means the use of weak points to solidify your values, strengthen your will, and improve your ability to communicate who you are to the world.

Any place in your life where you feel unsure, or weak, or indecisive, you can make into a strong point. You can do it every time.

The extent to which you have been weak is the extent to which you can be strong.

Let's begin with your mind.

Chapter One: Mind

The wheels of your psychology.

"We are in the hands of those gods, those monsters, those giants: our thoughts."
– Victor Hugo

"Repetition is the father of learning. Intelligence… all that comes from repetition. Awareness, preparation… all that comes from repetition. Money, [nice ladies]… all that comes from repetition."
Rotation, record spins, repetition.
– Lil Wayne

What Your Mind Is

There's a difference between your brain and your mind. A good way to understand this difference is to think of a computer. Your brain is the motherboard, hard drive, memory card, and any of the other physical circuitry. Your mind, however, is the user interface—the keyboard, the touchpad, the screen, and the operating system.

These words on my screen are real, yet invisible. They're a projection of the computer's hardware.

Likewise, your brain is the physical structure that causes the mind, which is your sensation of the brain. Since it is your sensation of the brain, it is the conduit by which you interact with the brain.

I am a therapist, so this section is about your mind, not your brain. A neuroscientist can tell you about your brain. But knowledge of the motherboard doesn't help you use the computer any better.

Conscious and Subconscious

Your mind is made up of two parts: the conscious and the subconscious.

The conscious mind is that which you are aware of. If you are attentive to these words, then this sentence is in your conscious mind right now.

The subconscious mind is that part of your mind you are unaware of but can still access.

Let's take the thought of a skyscraper. You probably weren't thinking about skyscrapers before you saw that word, but now you are. The thought of a skyscraper was in your subconscious mind. When you saw "skyscraper," your brain immediately went to its skyscraper folder, which holds everything you know about skyscrapers.

That's the best way to think of your subconscious—as a filing cabinet full of folders that contain information about various subjects. Specifically, your subconscious is like a two-drawer filing cabinet. The files come in through the form of thought, observations, perceptions, ideas, action, or anything else you can be conscious of. When they come in, they go in the top drawer of your subconscious. This top drawer contains your subconscious thoughts.

Most thoughts go in and out. You learn, see, and hear, and it goes into your subconscious mind. But since you never think about it again, it goes out.

But some thoughts and observations stay in your top drawer. You continue to think about them or this new thought, this new file, relates well with the other files in your subconscious. It has a lot in common with what's already in your drawer, so it gains importance, in which case, it becomes a folder.

If you're an architect, your "skyscraper" folder is gigantic. It's full of files on a lot of other buildings as well. If you're a programmer, your file on skyscrapers is sparse, and so is your folder that contains skyscraper. Instead, you're full of folders on logic and symbol files—the ones you use regularly to program software.

The bottom drawer of your subconscious contains your emotions. Your emotions are your values and beliefs, which are thoughts you care about. They are thoughts linked up to many other thoughts and placed in a folder under the same meaning.

Whether a file goes into your second drawer is determined by three factors:
1. How well the file links up to other files and folders,
2. How well the file links up to your values and beliefs, and
3. How often the file remains in focus, which is usually determined by the above two factors.

If you're a programmer, an article on skyscrapers may amuse you, but chances are you won't retain much of it. It'll be a good article to read to pass the time on the subway, but nothing more.

However, if you're an architect, you may all but memorize the article. For you, that article isn't just about skyscrapers—it's about your livelihood, which includes how well you can provide for your wife and family. Each word for you represents food for your children.

This is your mind, and this is all your mind is. These principles are elaborated in Daniel Kahneman's *Thinking Fast and Slow*, and I will elaborate on these principles throughout this section, but the essentials of your mind are here.

Therefore, the extent to which we have a healthy mind is determined by whether we're aware of what's in our subconscious, and whether the files can help us achieve what we want.

It's no different than when a company's administrative staff audits its client files. Get rid of any files for clients you no longer have and update the existing ones.

Why the subconscious matters: The subconscious is the seat of our emotions, and emotions control what we do and how we do it. They control what we say and how we say it. Men who have lost function in their limbic system, the part of the brain that houses emotions, cannot even decide what to order at a restaurant. The concept of decisions or whether to make a decision baffles them.

Emotions are, effectively, in control of our entire life.

If we want to direct our life, we need to direct our subconscious. Specifically, we need to build our subconscious.

How to Build Your Subconscious

Now that you know what the subconscious is and why it's important, let's learn how to build your subconscious so it will do what you want.

Your psychology is Formula One racing, and you are in charge of the team. You decide how to build the car, which is your subconscious mind.

(I know I just likened your subconscious to a filing cabinet, and that is the more scientifically apt analogy, which I will explain later. But the Formula One analogy will help describe how to build your subconscious. Plus it adds another point of reference, which deepens our comprehension.)

The car is mostly in control, but you are in control of the car. The same is true of your subconscious. When you tell yourself it's time to go to the gym but instead you stay home and watch reality shows, that's your subconscious in control. Whenever you want to talk to a girl but instead walk quickly by her with your eyes trained on your shoes, that's your subconscious in control. You feel like you're out of control because in that moment, you are. But you are in control of your subconscious—or at least you can be.

To be in control of your subconscious, you must first build your subconscious. Here are seven steps to do this:

1. Figure out what you want
There's no such thing as a "best" subconscious. A subconscious is as useful as it is built for what you want it to do. There is a best "doctor" subconscious, a best "fiction writer" subconscious, a best "salesman" subconscious—but they will all be different. When you build a car, you can either give it high top speed or quick acceleration, but not both. It depends on what you want it to do.

The only incorrect way to build a subconscious is to have it do too much at once or nothing in particular. You cannot build a subconscious to be funny, and also build that same subconscious to get along with your mother-in-law. And if you build your subconscious to "like, be famous and stuff," you will end up as an Uber driver.

2. Focus

Once you know what you want to achieve, you need to control what enters your subconscious accordingly. This is done by your conscious mind, which is you, the team leader. The conscious mind can only hold limited amounts of information at once. But if you can focus well enough to play Nintendo, then you can focus well enough to build your subconscious.

Your subconscious is a genius with no will power. It is capable of more than you could imagine, but it only works well if it is given specific orders.

If you were to give a direction to your engineers, you would get a better job done out of them if you gave them specific instructions. If you just told your team to, "Oh you know, find some tires and put them on the body there, then make the car go fast," you would get a worse result than if you were meticulous and knowledgeable.

With specific instructions, for a specific purpose, you will get a better performance out of your team, ie your subconscious.

3. Fill your subconscious with good information

Part of what it means to focus is to learn all the time. Constantly, for a specific purpose. This can either be through experience or through books. If you want to be a journalist, learn everything you can about writing, politics, psychology, and the world (books), and also apply this information in any capacity (experience). Good information is out there, though probably not at journalism school. What is at journalism school, however, is other journalists. People are wealth. This is the extent to which college is useful, but it's an awesome extent.

4. Think in essentials

It's not enough to fill your subconscious—you need to build it, after all. This entails integration, ie the arrangement of information. Your subconscious is built well when similar bits of information are grouped together. What determines whether two pieces of information are similar? Their essentials, ie their fundamental cause. This is pattern recognition, which is general intelligence or IQ. When you think in essentials, your subconscious will be much more useful. You'll be able to retrieve the more-relevant information faster, create abstractions, and properly integrate new information.

Let's say you attend a lecture about Alexander Dumas. If you don't think in essentials, then you will link Alexander Dumas with your buddy named Alex, because all you take away from the lecture is the name—something unessential to what Alexander Dumas is.

Or, you could think of Alexander Dumas as a French author, in which case you will link him up to your folder for John Paul Sartre. This is more fundamental to what Alexander Dumas is, so it's more relevant, but there is little in common between Dumas and Sartre aside from the fact they are both French.

To better categorize, or integrate, Alexander Dumas would be to classify him as a 19th Century writer of the Romantic movement. Then, you will put him in the same folder as Victor Hugo, an author who he shares many similarities with. They have similar themes in their novels, they were both influenced by similar people, and they're entombed in the same room in the Pantheon. Yes, they happen to share a similar nationality, but this is only secondary.

When we think of Alexander Dumas by his essentials, we group him in our mind better, and so we allow for a better retention of him and what he is. As a result, we are able to understand both him and the world better.

5. Become aware of uncomfortable emotions
Your uncomfortable emotions are the parts of your Formula One car from last year that broke down at Monte Carlo. So you need look into your un-

comfortable emotions, most notably anxiety, anger, and their corollary, shame. Unpack them, see what's in them, and learn from them. This is the only way you can free your mind of them, and so free your mind of obstacles. It's impossible to build a new fuel injector around an outdated fuel injector. Sure, that old fuel injector may have served you well for a while, but there are new goals this year, and so new specifications.

6. Talk about emotions
The alleged reason why men don't want to talk about emotions is because we're afraid it will make us weak. The politically-correct response to this is it's okay for men to be weak, and any admonishment to be strong is merely a social construction. The truth, however, is it's completely reasonably for men to fear weakness. As it's reasonable to fear obesity and poverty—both are states that place us and the people we love in a precarious situation. Though the avoidance of emotions makes us even weaker.

This situation appears to be a Catch-22—we need to talk about emotions to become aware of them and so emotionally strong, yet we become weak when we talk about emotions. The way out is to talk about emotions in a specific way. Thankfully, we already have a structure for emotions (see *Anxiety* and *Anger*), so let's apply this structure to their discussion. We'll elaborate on this in a few pages when we discuss introspection, but for a discussion of emotions, keep two principles in mind: connection and responsibility. We take responsibility for our emotion and use it to connect with others. We don't blame others for either our situation or emotion, and we talk with the intention that other people will be able to relate with us.

7 Take action
The best way to access and change information in your subconscious is through action. Information is more than your perceptions, knowledge,

thoughts, and feelings. Information is action; action is information. Thus, "learn by doing."

Let's say you want to be a better public speaker. What you would need to do is infuse the thought "I am comfortable speaking in front of others" somewhere deep within the second drawer of your subconscious. If this one thought, this one belief, was lodged deep in your subconscious, in the back part of the bottom drawer, then it would infuse all the other folders ahead of it, and so infuse much about you.

It's difficult if not impossible to put this thought in the back of the bottom drawer of your subconscious simply by thinking the thought in there. This is the attempt of hypnosis and neuro-linguistic programming, both of which are like corporal punishment for your mind, and like corporal punishment, only work in the short-term and aggravate the problem long-term. Instead it's more helpful to first process unconscious insecurities, then practice public speaking. Through an engagement with the issue as it is, instead of an attempt to cover it up, you imply to yourself, on a deep, emotional level, over and over again, you speak comfortably in front of others.

Action is the most effective way to access and change the bottom drawer of your subconscious.

Unlike thoughts, actions tend to deposit in the second drawer of your subconscious. Since action is emotional, you typically will not take an action unless it's based on a file or folder deep in your subconscious. So when we are able to will an action without a file there to support an action—or even in the face of a contradictory files—you put those files there, and so cause a deeper change than you can affect by mere thought.

In a way, however, action is a thought. A conscious action is a thought you tell yourself, and subconscious action is a thought revealed to you.

The action becomes even more powerful—even more transformative—when you use the unhelpful folders of the second drawer of your subconscious as the basis for your action. This is what you do when you confront your anxiety—you open up the anxiety folder, which releases energy, then use the energy to do the opposite of what the folder tells you to do. It's painful but it's possible.

Your anxiety folder probably has the file "I'm not good enough to speak in public," and when you feel that file to in fact speak in public, you not only get rid of that file, but you replace it with a new one that says "I am good enough to speak in public." You, in effect, use the energy of that which works against you to work for you. It's the same principle behind jiu-jitsu.

Thoughts and Identity

As a thought stays in the first drawer of your subconscious, it may attach itself to more and more thoughts through repetition and integration. Now these thoughts "fire" in unison when one of them is triggered. This is the thought as it becomes part of a folder in the bottom drawer of your subconscious. Folders in the bottom drawer of your subconscious, when activated, influence a much larger portion of your brain. Folders or files in the first drawer, when activated, influence a smaller portion of your brain.

Let's look at an example to see how this works. You grow up in a religious household and you learn, from an early age, that God created the earth 6,000 years ago. At first, this is a thought, nothing more. But it gets repeated over and over and so stays in the first drawer of your subconscious. The longer it stays there, the more the idea becomes associated with other ideas, like your community, your love for your father who is religious, and your love for your Sunday school class. Gradually, since the idea the earth is 6,000 years old is linked to what is important to you, the more that file becomes lodged deep in the second drawer of your subconscious.

Then, when you go to college and learn the earth may be 4.5 billion years old, you will have a difficult time accepting it. This isn't because you're dumb—this is because, due to the nature of your mind, it will not accept information that contradicts something important to you. Not right away, at least. This one idea does more than threaten your thought about the age of the earth—it threatens your friendships, your family, your view of life, and so your psychological stability.

To incorporate this new idea, you will need to, in effect, incorporate a new identity.

Want and Need

The discrepancy between the conscious and subconscious causes the discrepancy between needs and wants. The conscious mind tells us what we need to do, and the subconscious tells us what we want to do. Since decisions and actions are rooted in the subconscious most of the time, the subconscious tends to win out.

To build our subconscious and so master our mind means to sync up our subconscious with our conscious. This way, our wants and needs become one.

Let's take an average, 20-years-old guy as an example. Like most 20-year-olds, he's lazy. His subconscious is filled with many "lazy" files. They may not tell him explicitly to be lazy, but they do tell him to "be cool" and to "chill out" and to "have a good time" because "work is not that big of deal anyway." And "remember that one cool skater guy in high school who got all the girls? He was too cool to work and be productive, and that's why all the girls liked him."

But around 20 years old, he begins to feel the need to work on his career. He's failed a few of life's challenges and experienced fear. Now his conscious mind tells him to work harder, but his subconscious mind still tells him to be lazy. If he wants to grow—that is, if he wants to change the files of his subconscious—he will need to make conscious decisions.

This will include the incorporation of all the steps of subconscious construction, which is a process that's as difficult as it is simple.

But as he replaces the lazy files with productive files, what he needs to do gradually becomes what he wants to do. His files and folders that tell him to work lodge themselves deeper in his subconscious. His decision to work, in effect, becomes easier. Eventually, it becomes the default.

This process also takes place when men talk to girls. The fear of girls is, far and away, the biggest fear of modern men, based on my experience. I've worked with veterans who've had bullets whiz by their heads who, for the life of them, cannot talk to a girl in a coffee shop. These men must have a lot of files in their subconscious that tell them to avoid girls they don't know. This is what they want to do (and do), because it's a dominant message from their subconscious. What they need to do, of course, is to first process their fear, which mostly takes the form of insecurity, and then talk to more girls. Only this will replace those files in the second drawer of their subconscious with more helpful files. Eventually, they will want to confront this anxiety, which becomes as natural as girl avoidance is now.

This explains the process behind *Anxiety* and *Anger*. In those parts of this book, I don't advocate the removal of anxiety, and I definitely don't advocate you ignore it because "it's all in your imagination anyway," as the cognitive hegemony and affirmation junkies profess. I explicitly indicate the use of the energy of your anxiety and anger to propel you to growth. When you use the energy of the anxiety and anger to build a constructive habit, you replace the files in the bottom drawer of your subconscious in one fell swoop.

In your "be lazy" folder, a piece of paper could say "you look like a dork when you work hard." When you hold the "you look like a dork when you work hard" paper in your conscious mind, you're more likely to see it as silly. As you become more self-aware, you in effect look at each individual piece of paper to see how it contributes to your folder, and how the folder contributes to your actions. Then, when you work hard while aware of the paper, you more fully replace the paper.

Want *vs* Need

This is a simple process if difficult. But often it doesn't appear simple. The question I get asked the most is, "how do I tell the difference between a want and a need?" Since "want vs need" appears in several titles of my podcast episodes, and since I cover this in my "follow your bliss" video, I'll leave this section brief here.

First off, a want is a need. To think they're separate is a sign of a scarcity mentality and low self-esteem. Why else would we rationalize away something we want? We must believe on some level it's unimportant or a burden on the environment and so by consequence we're unimportant or a burden on the environment. The only difference worth discernment here is between an unhealthy need and a healthy need. The difference is a healthy need increases pleasure, or happiness, and an unhealthy need decreases pain. It takes a decent level of emotional regulation to discern between these two states. Confront that anxiety, assert that anger, then learn what you can and adjust accordingly. Simply the knowledge that there's an important difference between the increase of pleasure and the decrease of pain will put you on the right track.

The Nature of Change

When we learn how the mind works, it's easy to deconstruct the nature of change. Change is to rid the subconscious of the old files that do not serve us and replace them with new files that do serve us. That's it. The steps of how to build our subconscious are how we do this.

New file acquisition requires books and knowledge—this is the easy part of change. The more difficult yet permanent and so awesome part of change is the change of beliefs about who you are and what is possible for you. Ultimately, beliefs, or thoughts linked to emotion, are the foundation of action. There is nothing else you could act from.

Automatization

Change doesn't occur all at once. Sometimes it does, but not usually. Often, it takes a while to implant a new belief, thought process, action, or way of learning into your subconscious. When you do, the belief, thought process, action, or way of learning has become automatized.

For instance, when you were in the second grade you had to learn $6 + 3 = 9$ by counting it out on your fingers. But that slow process has long since been automatized, so when you see a 6 and a 3, you immediately make them 9.

This process is also evident as a toddler learns to walk. At first his movements are conscious, which makes him look like the town drunk as he stumbles about. It takes a lot of mental effort for him to walk. But the more he practices, the more it becomes automatic.

The process by which you solidify your values is no different. Your habitual thoughts and their patterns can be ingrained deep in your subconscious—the process has become automatized. For years, you've come home from work and watched two hours of television. This seems to happen automatically. But your cardiologist says there's plaque in your arteries, so now you need to go to the gym directly after work, which contradicts your subconscious.

This process causes frustration, so it's important to remember the frustration says nothing about you—it's simply how your mind works. When you replace an old process with a new one, keep in mind you're still that second grader who has to count out 6 plus 3 on his fingers. Nothing to take personally or get upset about, you simply need new files.

When we challenge the subconscious like this, conflict is inevitable—emotions will arise, the causes of which can be mysterious, confusing, or vague.

In order to get to the root of these emotions, to see what's in our subconscious, we need to isolate our emotions so we can look at them. To do this, it's helpful to employ introspection.

Introspection

Introspection is the process by which we turn emotions into words—that is, we turn the recesses of our subconscious into words. Emotions are composed of thoughts, ideas, values, and memories, and introspection is how to see what those thoughts, ideas, values, and memories are. Introspection is the way to access the subconscious, uncover its content, and see how it's connected. It is essential if we want to uncover and understand our values, see what we care about, and decide what to do.

I indicate introspection a little bit in *Anxiety* and *Anger*. We discussed awareness of our anxiety and anger through the acclimation to the emotion. This practice is important, but it's only a low-grade introspection. The process here needs to be further deconstructed to give us a firm grasp on what it means to fully regulate emotions, and not only sit with them. Introspection is a guided tour in emotional regulation.

Here are the six steps of introspection:

1. Identify the emotion

Hint, it will be either anger or anxiety, or some combination thereof. It's important to use your own words to describe the various shades of anger and anxiety. This makes the introspection personal, which is vital. Men often fall into the trap that tells them they need a specific outcome from introspection, or they need to solve a certain problem, or they need to feel a certain way. This moralization drives them in circles. Introspection is the opposite of this moralization—it's an identification of the subconscious for what it is.

2. Identify why you feel the emotion
Often, why we feel an emotion is more important than what we feel. This step is where you see what loss or threat causes the anxiety, or what need or injustice causes the anger. When you do this right, it feels like we put a pin through some thought that's been dancing around the edges of awareness.

3. Identify what makes this emotion personal
This is the most important step of the introspection. We not only look at the feeling, but what it matters in the context of our entire life. Maybe it means something because of how our authoritarian father used to make us feel. Maybe it means something because it's just like that one time we dropped a game-winning pass in high school football, and it cost the team a championship.

4. Ask yourself if you're correct
It's helpful to take a step back to wonder if what we've written in the first three steps is true. Consider what a friend would think about the situation and evaluation (or maybe even ask a friend). It's also helpful to assume the opposite of what we've written and see if it rings true. The introspection doesn't need to be perfect, but it does need to be honest, or at least as honest as possible. As long as we're as honest as we possibly can be, and we don't use the introspection to justify our emotions to ourselves, then the introspection is self-correcting.

5. *Take responsibility*
As we learned in *Anxiety* and *Anger*, the emotion isn't ours, or we cannot use it in a mature way, until we take responsibility for it. Someone else may wrong us, but our reaction to it is still 100 percent our responsibility.

6. *Summarize what you learned, and your next step.*
Write out what you learned as concisely as possible. You can usually get it down to one sentence, fewer than 30 words. Then think of a specific, concrete action to take as a result. It can be tiny—send an email, call a friend, ask a question. It's not important that you take a big step, as long as you take a definite, measurable step.

The next step may unearth a deeper conflict from which more introspection may be required, but we will only know this once we take the step. Remember, action reveals our subconscious to us.

Many guys fall into this trap: they begin the introspection with an idea of what their next step should be, and they go through the introspection to rationalize what they want to do. This will only decrease self-awareness while we think it increases. Only consider what to do after you've completed steps one through five.

Through introspection, we slow down a process that normally occurs instantly. When we slow down our process of introspection, we can do it more accurately, with better results.

And note that introspection doesn't entail we question what we feel. Remember from *Anxiety* and *Anger*—our emotions are always legitimate, but how we evaluate them and what we do with them is not always legitimate. So it's healthy to accept our feelings, but never blindly accept our evaluation of our feelings.

When you first begin introspection, it's important to write out each step. After a while, though, you may be able to do this process in your head as it becomes automatized. As you introspect more and continue to learn more about yourself and your values, you will be able to introspect in real time, in the middle of an argument, for example.

When we introspect in real time, this is when we really begin to take control of our life. People will be able to feel your presence from a mile away.

Introspection can do more than uncover disruptive emotions—given enough practice, it can uncover anything in your subconscious. So it's also helpful to use introspection if you want to uncover and clarify your values (which may be at the root of a disruptive emotion). The point is, there are files and folders in the second drawer of your subconscious. They're difficult to look at, but introspection makes it easier to look at them.

It's not your fault that you have disruptive, vague, or confusing emotions. But it is your responsibility to do something about them.

Let's end this section with the reminder that introspection takes practice, especially if you've become good at the repression of different parts of your subconscious because they're too scary to look at. But you will become better at it. If you want to incorporate introspection into your life, I highly recommend you do it along with meditation. When we let our mind go through its automatic processes without distraction, we in effect let the second drawer of the subconscious come to the surface. More on this and other self-awareness techniques in the next part on self-awareness.

We become the master of our life as we become the master of our subconscious.

Every Day
So far, we've covered the fundamental mechanisms behind psychological change—from your thoughts, to your actions, to how you look at your sub-

conscious and handle disruptive emotions. It's important to note that change doesn't occur overnight. And the only way I have found—and the research has found—to make permanent change is to do something consistently, every day, for 30 days in a row. At least 24 days, but preferably 30 days. Of course, 60 days would be better, and 90 days would be better still.

Whenever I see men who have undergone a deep, meaningful, permanent change, whether it's a habit, a personality trait, or even a worldview, it's always the same story: whatever they did, they did it every day. Not five days per week. Not six days per week. Every day. Sometimes for months or even years on end.

Stories from my life

I began talking to girls when I was 13-years-old. It started off as parlor trick in that it entertained my friends and we would take bets on whether I would get her number (I usually didn't). But it wasn't until I was 23 when I first talked to three girls every day for 30 days, that I became somewhat good at it. Since then, I've done this multiple times. And I've even done it 90 days in a row, and each time it felt like I got a new brain.

I noticed the same phenomenon when I went through a depression in college. I began to read the Six Pillars of Self-Esteem *by Nathaniel Branden, but it didn't make me feel any better, at least not at first. Then, when I happened to read the book for five days in a row one week, I noticed my outlook change. I noticed my thought process change. Then I read it every day, three times per day, for about five to ten minutes each session, and again, it felt like I got a new brain.*

A former roommate of mine was a comedian. You probably wouldn't recognize his name, but he has had side roles in A-list movies. And his advice for novice comedians corroborated what I knew—to fully acclimate to the stage, you need to get in front of an audience every day for six months. In fact, he didn't think a comedian had much of a shot if he worked any less.

Consistency, not intensity, is what it takes to remove files and folders from the bottom drawer of your subconscious and replace them with new files and folders. Save a mental breakdown, it's near impossible to replace thoughts and actions in one fell swoop, and even mental breakdowns don't work as well as consistency. In other words, I'd rather you introspect once per day (it takes about three minutes) for a month than sit down once per week for a marathon session of baggage revelation.

Intuition

There is an ability men have that judges what something is prima facie. We understand a lot about somebody by their clothes, their haircut, how they walk, talk, and make eye contact.

The ability to do this is called intuition. To paraphrase Carl Jung, intuition is the ability to decipher where a man has been and where he is going. Intuition works when we subconsciously recognize patterns in our environment, though we don't know the precise subconscious basis for these patterns, so it feels to us like a gut reaction.

Let's say you have known of ten guys who have all had neck tattoos, and they have all been known to lose their child support money at the track. Then you meet an eleventh guy who has a neck tattoo, and your intuition tells you he probably needs to go to jail at some point, if he hasn't been already. When you hear he has beat up his girlfriend, whose father also had a neck tattoo, you are not even a little bit surprised.

This is because you have registered files in your subconscious that relate neck tattoos with poor impulse control and violence. You didn't do it consciously, but you did do it.

Intuition is neither good nor bad—it depends on how accurate your intuition is, which depends on how accurately your subconscious and its connections reflect reality. We all intuit, so it's good to build your subconscious well to make intuition useful. Otherwise, you'll fall for a girl who downs five vodka gimlets on your first date only because "she was a lot of fun."

Throughout the history of philosophy, intuition has been considered a mystical, supernatural process. It has been used as a placeholder to explain how philosophers acquire knowledge in ways they do not understand. Philosophers like Plato, for instance, claim to know of an object in the world before he has sensed it. Plato and other philosophers have referred to this phenomenon of "just knowing" as supernatural because it feels supernatural to them. It makes sense it feels supernatural to them, but it is not. It's merely how your subconscious works.

The subconscious mind perceives when you do not think it perceives, and it makes connections when you do not think it connects.

If you don't understand how your mind works, then your intuition will of course seem mystical. Your subconscious is home to powerful processes. It controls everything about you, all the way from your worldview down to the flicker of your eye.

As a result, there is a split in our culture between reason and mysticism. How do we as humans acquire knowledge—through reason or through mysticism? But this split is unfounded, since mysticism is only an inaccurate placeholder for subconscious processes, which are indeed natural.

(This split has led to the philosophical divide between the liberals and conservatives in modern American culture. The former insists we do what we need to do, even if it doesn't work, and the latter insists we do what we want to do, even if it has no base in reason. They're two sides of the same coin, or to put it more accurately, two parts of the same mind.)

And since most of our decisions are subconscious, which includes our implicit decisions of perception, they bring us to conclusions we "simply know." It's easy to see how this process could be mistaken for mysticism, even when there's nothing remotely mystical about it.

Speaking of mysticism, let's talk about God.

What Is God

A supernatural God could not philosophically, by definition, exist. Yet I understand what people mean when they speak of God. It's a guiding force in life. It sometimes knows what we need better than we do. It is the awe and reverence for something we feel that's too vast to see, too complex to understand.

God, in other words, seems a lot like your subconscious. There are 100 billion neurons in your brain. The way in which your neurons can connect—which would be any combination of two or more of them—is effectively infinite. The number of permutations of your neurons would be roughly the factorial of 100 billion. When you type this into a calculator, all you get is infinity.

Even the factorial of 1000 is a number with 2500 digits. Googol only has 100 digits. The number of atoms in the universe has 82 digits. So even if your brain had only 1000 neurons, the number of possible combinations of them—each of which would constitute a unique thought, feeling, perception, sensation, or any brain state—would still be exponentially greater than the number of atoms in the universe.

The collection of these 100 billion files, and however many permutations thereof, is my naturalist, psychological theory of what God is. We cannot know the extent of the ways in which they connect. All we can say is it's a powerful process, it controls your life, and you can build it.

Your subconscious is God; your focus creates God.

When men say their God is their master, this is a statement of profound psychological truth. They do not put themselves in the hands of some other realm, though that's what it seems like to them. They simply turn themselves over to another part of themselves, a more powerful part, because their conscious mind is not up to the challenge.

It's not a lie to say your mind is reflected in and a reflection of the universe. No more it's a lie when a mom tells her child babies are delivered by storks. Our conscious experience feeds our subconscious, and our subconscious feeds the permutation of neurons, and the permutation of neurons feeds our life.

It's easy to see why every culture has created a God—any being that tried to understand its subconscious through its conscious would create a God. Our puny conscious awareness cannot wrap itself around the universe that is our subconscious mind, so we simply say "God" or in fact now "Universe" and assume He, or It, is external.

It's easy to see why every culture's God reflected its own culture—culture created God. Or, to put it another way, experience creates the subconscious mind, and the subconscious mind creates God.

It's easy to see why Carl Jung's response to the question, "Do you believe in God?" was, "I don't believe in God—I know God exists." He understood if you get enough people together, they will create a God. God is human; the commandments of God are culture.

As the West has become more advanced, wealthier, and more peaceful, God has become less vengeful and more magnanimous. God has changed because we have changed.

I talk about God for perspective. If you feel anxiety about a new business venture, you may know you need to confront the anxiety to overcome it. But when you do confront your anxiety, you are now part of a process that directs and controls your life. You are much more powerful in your action and thought because now, it's not about your anxiety—it's a religious experience. God—or spirituality or religion—is the connection of disparate parts of your mind into one, unified whole. Then you receive the bounty of the gods—Enki of Sumer transcends dualism, Gilgamesh of Mesopotamia transcends time, Cai Shen of China transcends money. And Fred of Idaho breaks up with his girlfriend to write a novel, thus he explores the netherworlds of his mind. It's all the same story.

**God hasn't created you in his image—
you create God in your image.**

The Unconscious

There is another process of your mind called the unconscious, which is not only outside of your awareness (like your subconscious), but it is completely outside of your control. You die with the unconscious you were born with.

The unconscious regulates body temperature, controls heartbeat, informs temperament, and controls other processes like white blood cell production. It is also the seat of your pleasure-pain mechanism (which we will discuss when we talk about your boundary). It is the seat of any other mechanism we are born with, like our two innate fears: ledges and loud noises. Most prominently, it is the seat of the archetypes, postulated by Carl Jung, which is either a pattern of or predilection for a behavior.

Evolutionary psychologists make the claim certain emotions, like jealousy, are archetypal. What is archetypal, however, is a straight man's desire for women, so if we do feel jealous, because of latent neurosis, it will more likely be because of a woman.

What these psychologists do is look out at society, notice that most people feel jealous, concoct a few just-so stories for why jealously is evolutionarily advantageous, and conclude jealousy is a part of who we are. Maybe it is, but I doubt it. Jealousy is a manifestation of culture, and since culture is everywhere, scientists sometimes mistake it for biology. Psychologists can notice a phenomenon, but this doesn't mean they can decipher the mechanism behind the phenomenon.

Another example from *Anxiety* is our fear of snakes. We are not instinctually afraid of snakes; no newborn is afraid of snakes. But it is much easier to condition someone to fear snakes than it is to fear, let's say, a doorknob.

One way to think of the archetype is as a meme that has been repeated to such an extent throughout our evolution that it becomes part of our psyche. We do not descend from primates who didn't care about females. So those impulses have accumulated within us. But let's be crystal clear and distinguish these innate desires from how we choose to act—from our emotional responses to these innate desires. This is to say the unconscious is in control most when it comes to sex. Men desire women who show signs of health. One study showed strippers make more money in tips when they're ovulating than when they're on their period. It was a big deal and it won several awards. Does this information help you in any way? Not really. At most it's cute, which is the most evolutionary psychology will ever be.

Men are not built or destroyed by the unconscious. We are built or destroyed by our subconscious, or how we choose to manage the unconscious archetypes we are born with.

I refer you to my article, *The Limits of Evolutionary Psychology*, for my dismissal of the omnipotence of the unconscious.

There is even a case to be made that the unconscious is under your control to some extent, though not to the same extent your subconscious is under your control. The unconscious process called "getting your sea legs" is one example. When you're out on a boat for the first time, you will become woozy because your inner ear adjusts to the rock of the boat. You don't do this consciously, nor could you if you wanted to. You cannot think about the minute perceptions of the boat's motion. Your mind perceives the movement unconsciously. After a while, your inner ear adjusts, and you have your sea legs.

Similarly, if we lack experience with girls and are thrown into the choppy waters of a first date, we may feel woozy. Due to the disorientation, we may miss an opportunity to kiss her. But after enough confrontation of this experience, the opportunity presents itself, and we "just know" when to make the move. Though perhaps these "sea leg" situations are subconscious? It doesn't matter how we classify them. What does matter is how we manage them.

Next, we will discuss a subject that is implicit in how the mind works: decisions.

Chapter Two: Decisions

Grease the wheels of your psychology.

"Good decisions come from experience; experience comes from bad decisions."
— Mark Twain

"Between stimulus and response there is a space. In that space is our power to choose our response. In our response lies our growth and our freedom."
— Viktor Frankl

The previous section implies the function of a decision to build and utilize your subconscious. The decision to focus, the decision to think in essentials, the decision to make the effort to think about your subconscious. Even the decision to read this book about your psychology.

Nothing happens in your mind without a decision. There is no such thing as psychology without a decision. There is no such thing as being alive without a decision. Even a hippopotamus makes a crude form of decision, and therefore has a crude form of psychology, which could be summed up in a few paragraphs about territory, sex, and hunger.

A rock, however, doesn't make a decision. There is no rock psychology. So the lifeblood of psychology comes down to decisions.

If you want to feel more alive, make more decisions.

This is exacerbated by the fact that not only do you make decisions like a hippopotamus, but you make them freely, of your own will. If you are under the impression humans do not have free will, then whatever I say after this will fall on deaf ears. So let's dispel the notion of determinism, or the idea that free will doesn't exist, before we go any further.

***

The Case for Free Will
There is no proof for free will, only a validation of it. It must necessarily exist because to deny free will, you must employ free will.

Let's say you make the statement, "free will doesn't exist." To make that statement, you cannot use free will to make that statement since, according to you, free will doesn't exist. There must be some impulse within you, outside of your control, that makes that statement. A social condition compels you to make that statement. An economic condition compels you to make that statement. Perhaps your genes compel you to make that statement.

Then for me to argue against your statement, neither would I be the one who chooses to argue. Again, my argument would only arise from some impulse outside of my control. If we were wholly determined, we would not argue from decisions caused by ideas, but from innate thoughts and impulses.

If we do not have free will, then the argument about whether we have free will is nonsensical. Given such premises, there can be no argument about free will—or anything else for that matter—so the importance of psychology goes right out the window because every debate comes down to the "it is what it is" bromide. Psychology needs free will to be a legitimate field like a heart surgeon needs to acknowledge the existence of a heart before he can operate.

Aristotle made this point 2500 years ago, and he was ahead of his time. He was ahead of our time, too. This is called reaffirmation through denial, which states you cannot refute something that you must employ to refute it. (Likewise, you cannot deny the existence of existence. To make this denial, you rely on the existence of your words to get your point across.)

Simply through the purchase of this book, a conscious effort to learn about your psychology, you understand implicitly free will exists.

Back to reality.

***

Decisions Are Mostly Subconscious
However, it sure seems like free will doesn't exist, at least some of the time. We've all been in the situation in which we find ourselves doing something we don't want to do after we're already doing it. This is because, as we've already mentioned, decisions are emotional—that is, decisions are

rooted in your subconscious. You only control your decisions to the extent you control your subconscious. This is why it's important to learn about the mind before we learn about decisions. Otherwise, we may as well learn algebra before we learn arithmetic.

As we learned, you are not, nor will you ever be, in direct control of your emotions. But you are able to control your emotions indirectly. And if you lie out in the sun all day, every day, you will get skin cancer. You have no control over this. However, you can control whether you lie in the sun all day.

How Decisions Can Be Conscious

Conscious decisions are made with a focused mind. You will recognize a conscious decision from the simple fact you're aware of it. The ability to make a conscious decision, to make a decision with awareness, is colloquially known as willpower.

We can also make the conscious decision to let emotions influence us in a healthy way. This is the crux of *Anxiety* and *Anger*. Rather than allow anxiety to let us avoid a difficult situation, we can begin to look at it as a signal to confront a difficult situation. This requires we understand anxiety, and it requires we make a conscious decision with a focused mind.

The Decision to Focus

Psychological health begins with the decision to focus, the decision to concentrate our conscious mind on what we want to concentrate on. This, ultimately, is what we use to build our subconscious in the way we want to build it. We perceive, through the five senses (and I would argue, more) thousands of bits of information every second. Your mind, however, only has the capacity to see a small fraction of those perceptions, about five to nine bits of information. A typical view of a city street, with its sights and sounds and smells, has millions of bits of information.

All growth stems from a focused mind.

First and foremost, it's imperative to make the decision to focus. Our focus becomes our thoughts, thoughts become emotions, emotions become values, values become decisions, and decisions become life.

This is the nature of goal-setting. A goal gives you something to focus on, and it gives you something to integrate into your subconscious by way of your decisions.

If there's one point to take away from this part of the book, it's to make more decisions. The more decisions you make, the better decisions you make, with enough time and awareness. Even if you make bad decisions, this still fills up the subconscious with more knowledge that can help make your decisions better in the future. Without a purposeful decision, there can only be stagnation.

Don't make good decisions; rather, get good at making decisions.

Notice the importance of decisions is implicit in *Anxiety* and *Anger*. The worst thing you can do with either anxiety or anger is to make no decision, which accumulates as OCD or depression, respectively. It is even better to do something immature with anxiety, like complain, than it is to do nothing and automatically regress to obsessive thoughts and compulsive behaviors.

Autopilot, an Unfocused Mind

Though free will exists, this only means it can exist. LeBron is capable of a stellar game performance, but this doesn't make his performance automatic.

When your conscious is out of focus, what goes into your subconscious is determined by your environment. You accept what you see uncritically, and you are not even in charge of what you see. You perceive only the loudest voices and the brightest lights. This is colloquially called being on autopilot.

When a man unfocuses his mind, he may be said to be conscious to some degree, since he experiences sensations and perceptions. But he isn't conscious to the extent required to direct his actions and thrive.

Without focus, much of what you're conscious of will come from your subconscious. Old thoughts and emotions will continue to resurface. These gets reaffirmed into the subconscious.

When we do not focus, we'll never be in control of what goes in our mind, we'll never be in control of our actions, and we'll never be in control of our life. Life will be a semblance of the majority, of culture, of whatever we're told, even when we have no idea what we're told. We will accept what the majority believes, and so we will do what the majority does. We will assume the mind of the majority, and we will end up with the life of the majority. By definition, we will be average, and there's nothing we can do about it—until we decide to focus our mind.

To be out of focus is to be controlled by your past and your environment.

It is inevitable we will be controlled to some degree by our subconscious. But if we want to grow, it's important to focus on what we want to focus on.

Part of what it means to have a goal, to focus on one thing instead of another, is to define who you are. You must give yourself something to focus on.

To do this, your decisions and your mind work in unison to create your boundary, which is the third and final part of your identity.

Conscious growth

Conscious decision

Unconscious growth (Awareness):
Connection, Introspection, Responsibility, Emotional process, Intuition, Meditation, Dreams

Stagnation: Habitual, unconscious thought, feeling, and action

Conscious

Automization: Repetition, action, ritual, consistency, prayer

Subconscious (Personal unconscious)

Informs patterns

(Collective unconscious)

Conscious
Unconscious

Mind and decisions diagram

Chapter Three: Boundary

The appearance of your mind and decisions.

"He who every morning plans the transaction of the day and follows out that plan, carries a thread that will guide him through the maze of the most busy life. But where no plan is laid, where the disposal of time is surrendered merely to incidence, chaos will soon reign."
– Victor Hugo

"The mind gives a picture of the remnants and traces of all that has been. But expressed in the same picture is an outline of what is to come. Therefore, a man's behavior is determined less by his past than it is by his future."
– Carl Jung

The psychological boundary is how decisions and mind combine to interact with the world.

Recently at my book club, I tried to explain what a boundary is to my buddy. Here he was in our friend's cramped apartment in the East Village on a Saturday night, sober, immersed in 19th Century literature. Girls and beers poured into the streets a few stories below.

His presence at a book club that night made his boundary evident. He made the decision to study literature as opposed to a beer menu—or anything else for that matter. That tells me, himself, and everyone else, a lot about the contents of his mind, his values, his past, and his future.

Your boundary is the veneer of your mind and decisions.

Your boundary is what the world sees as you. It is a combination of all your likes and dislikes, and all of what you do and you do not do. The sum total of every single file in your subconscious, made visceral.

If a man works 12 hours per day to save up to start a family and take them on vacations, then that says something about his decisions and his mind. It is his decisions and mind made manifest.

This also works on a smaller scale. I prefer chicken wings to cheeseburgers, *Predator* to *Braveheart*, nature documentaries to reality shows, and lifting weights to cardio. My favorite author is Victor Hugo, and my favorite exhibit at the natural history museum—aside from the museum goers themselves—is the hall of human origins.

This is only a small piece of information about my boundary, but just from knowing these preferences of mine, you have a general impression of who I am—a meathead who tries to be smarter than he is.

These preferences make up my psychological boundary. They are the result of decisions I've made, how those decisions have affected my mind, and how my mind in turn affects my decisions.

You've probably heard of someone who has "crossed a boundary" before. This is when someone does something unacceptable to someone else—they impinge on who the other person is, either their decisions or their mind. Somebody who does this often without knowing it has boundary issues. Similarly, somebody who lets others cross their boundary without letting them know it has boundary issues.

To master your boundary, assert it quickly and with ease.

A Boundary Can Be Either Weak or Strong

The extent to which your decisions reflect your values, and your ability to communicate your values to the world, is the extent to which you have a healthy boundary.

A weak boundary is one that is undefined or poorly defined. A weak boundary represents an area of life you do not understand, or it represents an area of the world you do not understand. It could also represent an area you do not know how to handle due to lack of experience.

If you've never asked for a raise before, then chances are you have a weak boundary for that skill. You don't know what to do, so you ask others for advice to gain their knowledge and experience.

I have a strong boundary when it comes to philosophy. I can talk about philosophical topic at any time at any place with anyone, and I do it easily. I can probably get you to agree with anything I have to say on the matter. However, I have a weak boundary when it comes to fashion. When I shop alone, I'm helpless, and I need to ask somebody for advice.

We all have areas of weakness in our boundary. A weak boundary is a necessary part of growth. Like the growing Roman Empire, where it expands is where it's the most vulnerable. However, through new knowledge and experience about a weak area of your boundary, it can become strong.

Signs of a Weak Boundary

Since we all have a weak boundary to some degree, it's important to recognize its signs so we know where we could strengthen our mind and decisions. The following are the common signs of a weak boundary:

Worry: Worry is obsessive thought about something you cannot control, and never will be able to control, about the future. The hallmark of a weak boundary is the belief you control something you do not. Guys often worry about whether a girl likes them before they ask her out. But whether a girl likes you is not your concern—it's her concern. In fact, it is disrespectful to the girl to worry or even care about what she thinks.

In *Anxiety,* I define worry as anxiety over the future. And regret as anxiety over the past. Once you feel the anxiety, it's yours and yours alone to manage, but if you had a stronger boundary, you wouldn't even feel the worry or regret in the first place. You can begin to see here how one branch of your psychology affects another, which I'll lay out at the end of this chapter.

Chronic worry or regret without a specific object to feel worry or regret about is colloquially called stress.

Defensiveness: Defensiveness is when we react emotionally to a perceived threat as a way to protect who we are. We protect who we are because we sense our own fragility, and the mind does whatever it can to cover it up. The difference between a healthy defense and defensiveness is truth. Defensiveness manipulates others to see a false representation of who we are. To defend ourselves is to tell the truth, it is to believe the truth is the only defense required. The desired outcome of defense is truth—the desired outcome of defensiveness is self-protection.

"Unfair": Whenever this word is uttered, it's a sure sign of a weak boundary. It's an issue of acceptance. We think the world should be one way, but it isn't. The cause of this is the inability to accept or understand the world to be what it is.

Pop culture reference

Unfairness reminds me of Robert DeNiro's character in Taxi Driver. *Here is a guy who thought what Jodi Foster's character did was wrong, and he thought the world was unfair as a result. He thought she shouldn't hang out with creeps and lowlifes. Instead, she should be with a guy like him. His character had a weak boundary for Jodi Foster, and for situations similar to this.*

The belief something is unfair is intimately tied with anger, but your beliefs about unfairness lie in your boundary and how you see the world.

I often get asked the difference between unfair and unjust. Okay, I've been asked twice. The difference between an unfair situation and an unjust situation is knowledge and even conceptual thought, which is a topic for a philosophy book. If something is wrong because of an attempted manipulation of reality, then it's unjust. If something is wrong because it happens to not align with demands that may have no basis in reality, then it's unfair.

"Should" goes hand-in-hand with "unfair," but it's a common pitfall so it's worth noting separately. The word "should" is a marker for having a weak boundary: "I should make more money," "that girl should like me," "politicians should listen to me."

Need for approval: When you care about what others think of you, it means you do not have your own values and preferences solidified in your subconscious. You use the opinions of others as a placeholder—you must necessarily use the opinions of others as a placeholder. Nature abhors a vacuum.

Imagine an adolescent who does well in science and math. His parents push him to become a doctor because that would be a respectable profession. But the child is too young to truly come to his own preferences about who he is and what he wants, so he implicitly takes on the preferences, or boundary, of his parents. By the time he's halfway through medical school, it becomes near impossible for him to even make decisions about his life on his own.

Of course, we all care a little bit what others think of us. This is natural since we are, in part, social animals. But to care to such an extent that it takes control of our life is a sign of a weak boundary.

Comparison with others: When we're unclear about who and what we are, we inevitably look outside for verification from others. This leads to comparison. Though the apparent error is the comparison, this is merely a symptom of a deeper problem—the lack of value in our own life, or the inability to assert that value to the world as a function of a healthy boundary.

Manipulation: Our boundary delineates where our psychology ends and where the psychology of someone else begins. Therefore, when our boundary is weak, we will fail to make this delineation, and so we will want to control others. We micromanage and manipulate. We try to use our will on others instead of on ourselves. People have their own decisions to make and agendas to carry out—the most we can do to influence others in a healthy way is to develop gravitas (to be discussed toward the end of this part), speak to others with their self-interest in mind, and then let the pieces fall where they may.

Inability to say "no" and hear "no": Whenever we have a difficult time with "no," either its expression or impression, this indicates a weak boundary. Imagine a friend invites us to a party on a night we need to study, but rather than tell him we cannot go, we say maybe we'll meet him later. We have a weak boundary for this friend. To some extent, he is in control of our life.

Why are guys afraid of rejection? They have a weak boundary for any girl they find attractive.

When we're younger, in our adolescent phase, we may think the word "yes" makes people like us. This is how we're trained in a family structure. Our mothers didn't like it when we said no, but they liked it when we said yes. When we said no we become less a part of our mothers, and when we said yes we become more a part of our mothers, psychologically speaking. Thus we learn from an early age that acquiescence, especially to women, is how to make them feel good. It's a difficult habit to break because the bond with our mother releases chemicals similar to oxycodone.

Our mom's not at fault here, because this bond is essential for a while, but definitely not when we're 22 and go along with what a girl says (or what our boss says, or what our friends say) because it's a way to relive this heroin-response, mommy-love scenario from childhood.

When we're children, yes endears us to family and authority. When we're adults, no communicates respect.

I suggest to guys who have a difficult time with the existence of "no" and "girls" in the same scene to say no to whatever any girl asks for the next three months. Especially to a girlfriend or date.

"Can you pick me up from this party?" *No.*

"Can you help me study?" *No.*

"Can you take off my clothes?" *Not now. Maybe later.* (Hey, let's become strong, not eunuchs.)

Dishonesty: A reader once asked me if what we're dishonest about is what we fear. This is close, but incorrect. We're dishonest about that which makes us uncomfortable, and "uncomfortable" is another way to describe a weak boundary. We want to be a certain way—ie have a certain boundary—but we are not that way, so dishonesty is how we present in the way we want to be. Dishonesty is a smoke screen to cover who we are—it covers a weak boundary.

Vagueness: Often I get questions from guys who feel there's a problem in their life, but they're unclear as to what the problem is. They have a sense something is wrong, but they have a difficult time communicating it. They present a situation with no definitive question. The problem is vague. I can only infer what their true problem is. The reason for vagueness is a weak boundary. The solution to this problem isn't to solve the problem—rather it's to define the problem. Once we do this, a solution to the problem usually presents itself.

Your boundary delineates what's in your control and what isn't.

Projection: When we make judgments—either good or bad—about someone without adequate knowledge of them, this is a sign we have a weak boundary for that person.

An example from my life
I may tend to worship Victor Hugo at times, which means I take my good qualities and ascribe them to him. What I say about Hugo may be an indication of who I am or who I wish I was. As such, if Hugo resurrected and showed up in my life and asked me to do something, I would have a difficult time saying no.

Guys project onto girls and sports stars all the time. When we have incomplete information about someone, we tend to idealize them, especially if they're beautiful or have washboard abs.

Complex: A complex is when you have an emotional reaction to some thing or some event that takes you off of your keel. This can be referred to as a loss of composure, or becoming, as it's en vogue to say, "triggered." It's when many unwarranted issues and thoughts come up for you in a certain situation. A common example of this is when a guy becomes stilted in the presence of an authority figure, like a boss, professor, or policeman.

Rationalization: A rationalization is a lie we tell ourselves. When we get dumped by a girl who we're in love with, and she dumped us because we're a moron, we may tell ourselves we're too good for her anyway. Or we'll fabricate reasons why she was no good. This is often done in an upchuck of words like "bitch" or "whore." As with defensiveness, we rationalize to protect who we are because we sense our fragility.

Narcissism: People often confuse narcissism with a big ego. But the opposite is true. Narcissism is when we have no ego—ie a weak boundary—so we need the approval, validation, and attention of others to feel like we have a strong boundary. This only gives the appearance of a big ego.

I mention narcissism in *Anxiety* and *Anger* to describe a man who uses his emotions in a way that's destructive toward others—he either uses anxiety for helplessness, or anger for hostility. The cause of this, which is the manifestation of the inability to regulate emotion, is a poor sense of boundaries. We tend to impinge on someone else's boundaries when we have a poor sense of our own.

Miscellaneous signs of a weak boundary: Failure to speak up when treated poorly, needless giveaway of time and energy, covert contracts, feeling unappreciated or taken for granted, indecisiveness, guilty feelings when you take care of yourself or put yourself first, the belief self-sacrifice is noble, the over-sharing of life with strangers, the alteration of who you are based on who you're with, difficulty in the consideration of your own needs, a sense of emptiness.

Right now, you probably feel like crap because you realize the awesome extent to which you're an undeveloped manboy.

Join the club.

But as long as we become aware of our weakness we can, with practice, make it our strength.

How to Strengthen Your Boundary
Now that we know what we do wrong, here's a list of what we can do to create a more solid boundary. This will essentially be the opposite of the previous list, but it's worth an elaboration.

Be honest: As we stated, when we are dishonest, we in a sense communicate "I am not okay with myself." When we are honest about the weak spots in our life, we become more aware of them and therefore more able to strengthen them.

Make decisions: If you take nothing else away from *Identity*, take this: make more decisions. Pick where you go out to eat, decide where to meet, send that email, ask that girl out, apply for that job, start that company.

Make. More. Decisions.

Whatever you want to do, do it now.

Successful people have a tremendous ability to scan an environment or situation and come to a decision promptly of what to do. If it's the wrong decision, they learn from it and quickly move on to the next decision. To make a bad decision is infinitely better than a retreat to your Netflix cave. With new experience comes more knowledge, and with more knowledge comes a healthy boundary.

Define the problem: The biggest problem in our life exists because we have failed to define what it is. Introspection helps here.

Read: The more we know, the more we define values, and the more we can communicate those values to the world. The more we communicate and so receive feedback, either explicit or implicit, the stronger our identity will be.

Hear "no": A kind of therapy exists called rejection therapy, which is a game in which guys go out and, well, get rejected. They ask for a discount at a store, they ask for a raise, or they ask a girl out on a date. The point isn't to get any one of these things in particular—it's to get rejected.

The point is to have fun, yes, but it's also to firm up their boundary. Leave it to the unconscious of young men to initiate itself when no one else will.

When a guy fears rejection from girls, he in a sense says, "My boundary regarding girls is weak." The only solution, we now know, is to build our subconscious: process emotions, make more decisions, accumulate experience, and now hear the word "no" from girls over and over again. It's only in this way can we firm up our identity.

If you don't get rejected *every single day*, you're falling behind.

Say "no": This is the other side of the "hear no" coin. When you say "no," you communicate, "hey, here's my boundary." This doesn't literally involve saying no, but it could. It could mean we tell somebody what they're doing is lame, or it could mean we tell our friend we won't meet him at that party.

Remember:

To master your boundary, assert it quickly and with ease.

The Flexible Boundary

A boundary can become too rigid, which makes us lonely and miserable. This is when we cut ourselves off from other people and situations. A weak boundary is when other people or the environment has control over our boundary, and they let themselves in whenever they please. A flexible boundary, however, is when we have control over what gets in. The boundary lets in healthy people and situations, and it keeps out unhealthy people and situations. As we become more solidified in our values, and as we make more decisions, we will develop a flexible boundary. It's like a semi-permeable membrane on a cell—it lets in food and keeps out waste.

The Boundary Is Connected

In *Anxiety* and *Anger*, I discussed how, if we handle anxiety or anger in one area of our life, it will make it easier to handle anxiety or anger in another area of our life.

Let's say you want to ask out the barista at your local coffee shop, but you're anxious to do it. If you do it anyway—specifically through the use of the anxiety as fuel for action—you will be less anxious when you ask for a raise at work.

The same is true for our boundary since it's only a reflection of how we manage emotions. The more we strengthen one area of our boundary, the more likely we will be able to strengthen other areas of our boundary. The mechanism by which we strengthen our boundary is the same in every situation.

Imagine our boss piles work on our desk, more work than is our responsibility. The more we're able to say no to him, the more we're able to say no in other areas. Let's say we drink too much and "should" drink less. A no to our boss strengthens the no to the booze.

This is helpful to understand because if we have a difficult time with honesty, we can strengthen our boundary in other ways, which will make it easier to be honest.

Boundary Is Trust

When I was younger, I thought a girl liked a guy to the extent she got along with him. Whether this was through similar interests, activities, or morals. This is logical, which is a sure sign it isn't how life works when we deal with girls in a romantic context.

> *An example from my life*
> *As I got older, it seemed the more I disagreed with girls, and the more I asserted myself unapologetically, the more girls were at-*

tracted to me. Even when I asserted myself on our most divergent values. In fact, the more fundamental the value we disagreed upon, and the more I communicated who I was calmly and unapologetically, the more they liked me. It's interesting when a girl says she's religious, then I respond with something to the effect of, "Well I'm not a Christian, so I guess this isn't going to work." Her response here tends not to be what we would expect.

The point is girls don't care about what our boundary is so much as how strong it is. A girl would rather be with a guy who she doesn't get along with but at least has a strong, well-defined boundary, than with a guy who has a weaker boundary, but similar values.

Why? It's an issue of trust. Girls, and people in general, trust you, and so respect you, to the extent to which you have a strong boundary.

I'm reminded of a reader who emailed me about a girl he had lied to about his age. He was 27-years-old, but he said he was 24. He felt like he needed to lie to the girl about his age because she was 21.

He asked me if he should come clean and tell her his age, because as he thought, "whether I'm 24 or 27 isn't a big deal." Right, it's not a big deal, but the fact that you lied is a big deal. The girl doesn't care so much about your age. But what girls do care about is whether they can trust you, and if she knows you lied, even about something stupid—especially about something stupid—then she knows she can't trust you.

A strong boundary—ie the girl's ability to trust you—in a relationship is essential to the healthy function of a relationship. Therefore, a lie about your age is unsalvageable. You could come clean and she might say she forgives you, but there will be that seed of doubt, and the relationship will suffer in subtle ways. In this situation, it's better to break up—no matter how much you like her, and no matter how good you guys are for each other. Take solace in the fact that the hindsight pain of immaturity exists to make the lesson stick.

Another example that demonstrates the importance of trust is the psychological test. This is when a girl subtly finds out more about a guy who she may want to date.

If you had to find out whether someone was a liar, how would you do it? You couldn't ask them if they were a liar, because they could lie and say they are honest. So what you would need to do is construct a situation in which they would greatly benefit from dishonesty, and observe what they do.

Every female, God bless 'em, has a PhD in the construction of these blind tests that determine, ultimately, if we're okay with who we are. A common test for when we begin to talk with a girl is when she says, "So I bet you talk to all the girls like this," or "How many times do you do this per day?" Now, I could give a good line to respond to this with, but that would only be a pretense to a strong boundary. What's necessary if you want to be fulfilled is to develop a strong boundary, and then it doesn't matter what you say. You could have the cleverest comeback or no comeback at all, and it's all fine.

Tests don't only come from girls, of course. Everybody tests. Your boss tests, your clients test, your friends test. Usually the person with the more-defined boundary—ie the person who has the higher status—will test more in the interaction.

Our Boundary Is What We Get
Boundary is trust with other people, but it's also trust with the environment. In any given interaction, the man who has a strong boundary, and who is able to communicate it well, is the one who will likely get that boundary met. Another way to say this is:

Our boundary is what we get in life, most of the time.

The more clearly we can develop our boundary, and the more we can back it up with defined values, and the better we can communicate it, the more likely we will get our boundary met.

Culture is drunk on positive thoughts, affirmations, and goals. It has been for a while. Though we can see how such mantras and conscious requests are only as helpful as their context. We can make all the goals and repeat all the affirmations we want, but if our head isn't screwed on straight—ie if we have a weak boundary—none of it will matter.

We don't get what we want—we get who we are.

This becomes evident when you get to know rich guys. What's interesting about rich guys is they don't think being rich is a big deal—to them, it's natural. Wealth is what they expect from themselves. They expect to be rich in the way we expect to tie our shoes. They have a clear boundary when it comes to money, usually in the implicit form of "I need to make at least X amount." And because it's accepted as given by their mind, they make it happen as easily as you make tied laces happen.

The Nature of the Boundary
The boundary is our values, the product of our mind and decisions, so let's look at how our values relate with our two basic emotions, the two other branches of psychology, anxiety and anger.

This section could be an entire book in itself, but I'll do it in fewer than 500 words. Okay here we go… starting now:

All men come with an innate pleasure-pain mechanism (which is part of the aforementioned unconscious). When something is good and leads to more life and happiness, it becomes associated with pleasure. When something is bad and leads to less life and happiness, it becomes pain.

A value is that which is important to us. This could be a positive value, something to gain or keep, or it could be a negative value, something to avoid.

When enough files and folders get lodged in the subconscious that tell us to get a thing or to avoid a thing, then that thing becomes a value.

At a certain point in life—toddler age—we accrue enough files that tell us to get a certain thing. A certain board game, for instance, becomes a positive value. You have many files that indicate you're good at this board game, and the files may even generalize to indicate you're good at life. As a result, you want to play the game all the time.

This is where the rubber meets the road regarding our two, fundamental emotions:

We feel anger about a positive value we do not have. A bigger apartment is a need, but we do not have a bigger apartment, so we feel anger about this. Anger is our tool to get this value—ie boundary—met.

We feel anxiety about a positive value we have conditioned ourselves to avoid. There has been too much pain and suffering associated with attempts to achieve that positive value. These files of pain and suffering go into our anxiety folder.

We feel anxiety about a negative value. It is right to have pain and suffering about a negative value, so anxiety is the survival mechanism to avoid this.

In other words, anger drives us toward a value, and anxiety restrains us from a value.

As I mention in *Anger*, desire is anger we know how to handle.

As I mention in *Anxiety*, the tagline of anxiety is, "I can't."

This is why a mastery of anger is more important than a mastery of anxiety—because when we feel enough anger, it plows right through the anxiety. Anger can focus us on what we want, so whatever anxiety we may feel pales in comparison.

Desire crushes doubt.

A guy will wrestle with anxiety all his life, but he will not be able to confront it fully until he feels his anger. It's good for him to have a *Network* moment of "I'm mad as hell and not going to take it anymore," and so his anger drives him to confront his anxiety. Men don't become more confident, they simply become more in touch with their desires. This is a phenomenon I discuss in my article, *The Wrath of Winter*.

There, 480 words. Not bad.

Boundary Metaphor

The concept of the boundary may be difficult to wrap our minds around. I could draw a diagram of the boundary, but that may only make it more confusing.

Instead, we'll use a metaphor.

Think of your boundary like you would a boundary of a country. Like your psychological boundary, the boundary of a country is a border that's invisible, yet real. A healthy border accepts and makes certain transactions with other countries, transactions that serve the country's purpose. And it declines other transactions that would hurt the country. A country is healthy to the extent it makes good deals with other countries based on the country's subconscious values, or culture.

North Korea, Cuba, and Iran are unhealthy, from a psychological perspective, because their boundary keeps everyone out. They tell lies to cover up who they are, and they often impinge on the boundaries of other countries. It's the political form of borderline personality disorder.

Conversely, a country like India has an unhealthy, weak boundary with its neighboring country, Bangladesh. Many Bangladeshis, who are predominantly Muslim, have emigrated into India. This has led to an increase in terrorist attacks against the more peaceful Indians, who are predominantly Hindu. India, because of its weak border, has been taken advantage of by Bangladesh. Psychologically, this is the same as when we let a narcissist ruin our dinner party because we lack the strength to say no.

Switzerland is a country with a strong yet flexible boundary. There are situations it definitely accepts, situations it definitely doesn't accept, and situations where there's room for negotiation. Their border is controlled through the prism of their culture, or subconscious values. They care about skiing, banks, and cheese—if you want to share in their values, then they're happy to include you. If not, that's fine too.

Becoming "Firm"

A while ago, I received a question from a listener about how to become, as he put it, "psychologically firm." He has no idea what a boundary is, or how it relates to our decisions and mind, but he has a vague yearn for one. We all do. A starving child, with a yearn for nutrition, instinctively eats dirt and clay for its minerals—and a psychologically starving man instinctively yearns for strength.

There are men in life who have this strength, this firmness, about them, and men who don't. The men who do have it garner respect, from men and women, become leaders, make more money, and get what they want most of the time.

This makes sense when we recognize the essential nature of the boundary: Our identity is the keystone of our psychology, and our boundary is the keystone of our identity.

The guys without a firm boundary cannot have a fulfilling life. After all, without a boundary, they have nothing to fill in the first place.

The more we can make purposeful decisions, develop our mind, and so solidify our values, the firmer we will become.

But this is only what a strong identity looks like behind the scenes. For clarification and demonstration, let's see what a strong identity looks like on the surface. Then we will be able to strengthen our identity from the outside in, as well as from the inside out.

Chapter Four: Individualism

"Between animation and life there exists a subtle difference: the personality, the enormous *I*."

– Victor Hugo

Individualism is the extent to which our decisions create our identity. And collectivism is the extent to which other people and the environment create our identity.

Collectivism has dominated psychology since Freud, yet it's no contention that individualism is the fertilizer of a healthy psychology. In fact, a man's psychology is healthy to the extent it is based on individualism.

Individualism is the most consistent predictor of happiness, health, wealth, and life satisfaction.

What we have in *Anxiety* and *Anger*, and now what we have in *Identity*, are the psychological gears behind individualism.

Though we now understand how those gears work, and we have the tools to work the gears properly, it also helps to understand what our psychology can do.

In other words, if we know what individualism looks like, then we can inadvertently strengthen our identity, confront our anxiety, and assert our anger if we change what we look like.

We will also know what's expected of us from hereon out.

Intention

The combination of the contents of our mind and the power to make a decision is intention. This is when we use our values, emotions, and subconscious, and materialize them in the world. We make something real and definite out of what's in our mind. Intention is the lens through which we construct our mind, make purposeful decisions, and firm our boundary. All symptoms of a disconnected mind, indecision, and a weak boundary can be lessened through intention.

The more specific and clear we can be about our intention, the more powerful we will be as an individual. The desire to become an architect is one thing, but the extent to which we are specific about the intention is the extent to which we are an individual. What kind of job do we want to have in architecture? What kind of buildings do we want to design? What will be the style of the buildings we design? What is our philosophy of architecture? Why even have a philosophy of architecture in the first place?

We'll know our intention is definite when we can write it out in one sentence, a single thought, 33 words or fewer. It includes who we want to help and how we want to help them.

Our intention may change. After we use a certain building design for a while, we may change our mind or improve a skill and so begin to design in a new way.

The way intention changes over time is also evident in men's intention with women. When men are young, they want to sow their wild oats, so to speak. After this becomes a waste of time, they settle down with one woman. Both intentions are fine, as long as we're clear about the intention we want for who we are.

The opposite of intention is the acceptance of whatever comes our way. Nature abhors a vacuum, as we have said, so when we have a weak identity, our environment inevitably creates our identity for us. Our counselor chooses our career, our boss chooses our salary, our friends choose where to go to eat. It all sounds good to us because without intention, it doesn't make a difference either way.

We wake up one day to a life that doesn't feel like our own—and technically, it won't be our own.

It's even more powerful to create a vision of our intention. Vision is intention we feel. We can sense it, touch it, smell it. When we feel our intention, we prime our identity for the life we want, for the life that is becoming.

The more definite the vision, the stronger the identity must necessarily be—the identity becomes stronger to catch up to the vision.

Contribution

When most men use the word contribution, there's a connotation of self-sacrifice, like we owe the world something for our existence.

Self-sacrifice is never noble, and you don't owe the world anything. This idea is an atavistic organ of religion and Marxism. Self-sacrifice is an admission we cannot manage our emotions in a healthy way.

The true connotation of contribution is to cultivate significance for our work, which goes above and beyond an intention. Maybe the architect doesn't see a bridge as merely a bridge, but rather a way to connect people. Maybe he sees a bridge as a way to symbolize man's dominance over nature. Maybe he sees the bridge as a metaphor for that one time he went to a baseball game with his father and had one, serious conversation with him before he died three weeks later. To give our work contribution, to give it a reason behind the reason, will make it that much more powerful, and it will make us that much more powerful in work.

The man who works to connect people has the sheen of an aristocrat—the man who works to only build bridges has the wear of a workhorse. Contribution may not change what we do, but it definitely changes how we do it.

The founder of In-N-Out didn't want to only sell a good burger. He wanted to sell a sense of clarity, that life is simple. This simplicity and ease is palpable when you walk in any In-N-Out—three colors, simple menu, no fuss.

The founder was a Christian, and this is how he felt every morning when he read the Bible. To him, all of life's answers were in that one book. Whether this is true is immaterial—the point is he had a contribution beyond the sale of burgers he wanted to give the world.

Let's say you want to design clothes. Your intention is to build a business that serves 500 clients. For you, though, because you have the idea of contribution in mind, it doesn't end there. Why do you want to design clothes? Because for you, clothes are more than a cover for the body. They're communication. Not only to others but to yourself. When you wear the correct clothes for you, you tell others and yourself that you're someone to be taken seriously. You're someone here to offer value. To create something from nothing. You're the hero's journey in 400 thread count.

When you outfit a client with the appropriate pocket square, you do much more than give him a pocket square. That accessory is a brush stroke on the mural of his contribution. A man who enters into fashion with such ideas of contribution—no matter how highfalutin—will do much better work, and be much more powerful. His individualism—and so his mind, his decisions, and his boundary—will have a perpetual source of nourishment.

Nowhere is contribution more important than with girls. A lot of guys go out into the meet market with the connotation of, at best, "Well I'm a good guy and I make a decent living, let's get together and try to have fun." That's weak. Girls feel the lightness of that—like it could be dispersed by a lull in the conversation. Why do we want a girlfriend? What deeper reason can we give? Maybe it's to grow, to help each other grow because we grow more in the presence of another. Maybe it's to give this girl a masculine force so she can be more comfortable with her feminine, pliant self.

Contribution connects your world and everything in it to the deeper parts of your psyche—and to the deeper parts of the psyche of others. This connection is the essence of religion, so there's no reason every building we enter cannot become a temple simply by how we choose to act in it.

Gravitas

The final stage in the development of individualism is gravitas. It's seriousness. It's heaviness. When we have gravitas, we're grounded, no matter what happens around us. We possess a steady persistence to life. People sense gravitas and so they naturally, well, gravitate to it. Companies are built around gravitas alone. The people close to us challenge us less, and "competition" becomes a word that used to mean something but we cannot remember what.

To understand gravitas, think of the Amazon River. It's much more than a single river, like the Nile. The Amazon River basin is comprised of countless tributaries and estuaries, all of which flow into the main river.

We have the main river of our life—intention—and everything else in life serves that intention. Our girlfriend serves that intention. Our friends serve that intention. The books we read, the people we spend time with, and even how we walk down the street. Everything we do and think and say is chosen to serve the intention, or it's the natural outcrop of intention.

Gravitas is respect for time—it is the only antidote to the fear of old age and death.

Gravitas is respect for the present moment—it is the only antidote to worry, regret, jealousy, and revenge.

Gravitas is respect for who we are—it is the only antidote to a life unlived.

Conclusion—Slay the Dragon

Stories work through symbols. When a hero slays a dragon, it's not a story about a hero who slays a dragon. The dragon is a representation of our unruly nature. The hero, by slaying the dragon, puts a pin in it. He doesn't kill it, necessarily—he sticks it to the wall like how we collected insects in grade school and stuck them to a poster board. Then we can point to it and say, "Look, there it is." This way we can observe it and understand it, so we can use it, instead of it using us.

This is my intention with this book—to slay the dragon, to put a pin in your psyche. Slow it down, point to it, look at it, and learn from it. To bring a clarity to our deep, murky issues—a clarity we previously couldn't even conceive as possible.

As the hero's battle isn't with a dragon, but an inner battle, the prize of the battle isn't glory, but an inner prize. The prize always is, and always has been, an ever-growing expansion of consciousness—new knowledge, belief, perspective, and a deeper connection with reality. That's all any man has ever wanted.

When we apply the materials in this book to slay our dragon, we begin to know, on a deep level that, no matter what happens to go wrong, we can get help from our psychological resources—our anxiety, anger, mind, and decision. An inner sense of security develops as we realize everything we have ever needed rests within our boundary.

Then we think and act from another realm. We transcend duality with Enki. We transcend time with Gilgamesh. We transcend money with Cai Shen.

It's here, with the idea of transcendence—of transcending the self—where we will continue and complete the unification of psychology in the fourth and final part.

Part IV: Self-Awareness

*The foundation of psychology
(or how grow by seeing yourself for what you are).*

"He who looks without, dreams—he who looks within, awakes."
– Carl Jung

What Self-Awareness Is

Self-Awareness is the ability to see who and what we are. That is, both the ability to see who we are in the present moment and in the context of our life.

Prima facie, this is a silly endeavor. We're already aware, right? Except merely because we can look at who we are doesn't mean we can see ourselves. As Sherlock Holmes admonishes Watson, "You look, but you do not see!" It's the difference between the ability to hear someone and to listen to what they have to tell you.

To look only requires eyes and perception, to see requires thought and conception. It's to understand our thoughts, emotions, and actions—where they come from and how they create our life.

It's this ability that's the foundation of psychology, the foundation of our identity, anger, and anxiety.

We may have been born with the faculty for self-awareness, but that doesn't mean it comes naturally. As the product of four billion years of evolution—the most powerful process man can conceive—we are a large, intricate organization. And any large, intricate organization will do whatever it can to protect itself when threatened. Not only physically, but psychologically.

Governments, companies, and churches do the same. Once they reach a certain size, they will unconsciously blind themselves to their faults in order to continue to exist as they are. This is why we get the Penn State child sex scandal—an institution becomes too powerful to be slowed down by a few misdeeds.

It's the same when our girlfriend breaks up with us for being a loser, and so we come up with ways to cover up the reasons why we're a loser. We won't consciously do it, but we'll call her a few bad names, only focus on our good traits, and then get drunk.

As churches need reformations, governments need revolutions, and companies need restructuring, we need self-awareness. Lies and cover-ups anesthetize our psychology, which may feel good—or at least not bad—until the overwhelming evidence of reality compels us to get our act together, which usually takes the form of incredible pain.

Self-awareness is a revolution in the psyche. It dismantles the layers of lies we've told ourselves to perpetuate a false conception of who we are.

If we commit to the revolution, we endure truths that will devastate who we think we are. But the main determinant in whether a revolution is successful is how bloody it is. Horror, as we will learn, puts us in contact with reality so we can do what we need to do.

The Purpose of Self-Awareness

I once asked my professor if there has ever been a book written on self-awareness. She took a beat, then gave me a dumbfounded look and replied, "No, I guess there hasn't been."

Turns out she was wrong, but the point is books about self-awareness are few and far between, plus they're unpopular. In fact, I found out later that another one of my professors had written a book about self-awareness, and even though he received his PhD from Harvard, he still had to self-publish it. (Technically, though, I would argue his book isn't about self-awareness—it's about mindfulness, a buzzword for focus, which is only a fraction of what self-awareness is.)

In a way, though, all psychology books are about self-awareness. Psychology is the study of man's relationship to himself, so psychology is implicitly the study of self-awareness—we cannot have a relationship with someone we don't know. But there has been little written specifically about self-awareness, about how to see who we are—about how to transcend the predilection to protect ourselves to see who we are.

Why? Probably for the same reason most books about beer aren't about why beer is fun—it's too obvious to merit explication. Yet self-awareness is crucial to understand our psychology because awareness is the inception of all growth. This is obvious when we think about it—if we don't know what to change, how can we begin to change it?

Self-awareness is tricky because its development requires the use of the very faculty we want to develop. We have no choice but to rely on our self-awareness to become more self-aware. It can be touch-and-go, to say the least. It's why a house appropriations committee may tend to tack on a congressional pay raise to their recommendations.

So think of self-awareness as you would a scientific theory. Technically, we are only 100 percent certain of a theory in a specific context of knowledge. But there are steps we can employ, like the scientific method and measurable observation, to ensure we develop a theory that adheres most strongly to reality.

Likewise, we can never be completely sure we're self-aware. But there are ways to think about self-awareness and steps we can take to ensure we're as aware as possible, given what we're emotionally ready to handle.

In the first chapter of this part, we'll cover how to think about self-awareness. In the second chapter, we'll cover the specific steps we can take to be as self-aware as possible. And in the third chapter, we'll look at cases from five of my past clients to demonstrate how to apply the unification of psychology to practical problems.

Chapter One: Theory

How to Think About Self-Awareness

"Diamonds are found only in the dark bowels of the earth; truths only in the depths of thought. It seemed to Jean Valjean that after descending into those depths, after long groping in the blackest of this darkness, he had at last found one of these diamonds, one of these truths, and he held it in his hand; and it blinded him to look at it."

– Victor Hugo

The History of Self-Awareness

Four billion years ago the earth was a mass of primordial goo. Every bit of matter and energy that exists today existed then, but it lacked cohesion. The protons, neutrons, and electrons mostly formed hydrogen, helium, carbon, nitrogen, and oxygen. Carbon, because of its inherent stability in the formation of bonds with other elements, constituted the backbone of the largest and most complex groups of elements.

By an event that's intuitively doubtful yet statistically probable, some of these carbon-based molecules began to make copies of themselves. Thus you were born. You were more prolific and accurate at making copies than other molecules, so you were more able to make more copies, and your copies were more able to make copies of themselves in turn. Perhaps this was because of an advantage inherent in your structure; perhaps it was because you were better suited for the environment—probably a little of both.

But your copies weren't perfect—otherwise you'd still be a molecule, forever making exact copies of yourself.

Through random variation, you evolved as a molecule in ways that are anything but random. Some copied molecules inadvertently ended up as more stable, and so you became even better at making copies of yourself. Your molecular offspring were therefore more stable, and so ever more able to make stable copies of themselves.

This is how you developed the ability to build a protein-based carrier around your replication molecules, to protect them. This gave you the premonitions of a body and a system of electrical impulses to receive signals from your body. You were then able to interact with your environment. As such, you necessarily changed your proto-body to be more adapted to your environment. Your mind and body were built together, and so they evolved together—one inseparable from the other.

After one billion years of this evolutionary process, you were something of a small worm who swam in the ocean. You had developed a mouth, or the premonitions of one, and you also developed the premonitions of an eye. For the first time you have the capacity for some kind of an awareness. Your growth now depends on your awareness of food in front of you. Now you need to detect food and swim after it, rather than let it inadvertently bump into your proto-mouth. Consistent improvements in locomotion and sensation made you into a fish after another billion years.

For the next billion years, your ability to sense food developed. Your eyes became better equipped to sense light and distinction between objects. You developed taste from a distance, or the ability to smell variances in your environment. And you became able to feel motion in the water. These increases in awareness added to the first of many explosions in the size of your brain. Your brain grew to support your growing need for awareness.

Then about one billion years ago, you began to crawl up on land. No one knows why you did this. Maybe it was for food. Maybe it was to escape predators. Maybe it was for no better reason than you felt like it—after all, by this point, you had the sensory and mental capacity to at least appear curious.

Since you were now able to survive on land and in water, you looked like something of a guppy. You still had gills to breathe oxygen in the water, but you also developed an air sack, the precursor of a lung, to breathe oxygen in air. As the atmosphere of earth became filled with more oxygen and nitrogen (conducive to your emergent lungs) you left the ocean forever. It didn't leave you, because salt water still flows in your veins as blood.

Now on land, you developed forelimbs and hindlimbs. It was a natural progression because you already had the fins for it. But you still moved side to side, like the fish you are. This atavistic movement used large amounts of energy. To make your way on terra firma, you had to develop a new way to move. So over the next several million years, your legs went underneath you and your body rose up off the ground. This ability to support this new body placement required much more coordination and balance, which led to another explosion in the size of your brain. And because you were off the ground, you had a greater ability to look up and down and side to side. When your awareness increased—when it had to increase given the demands of the environment—your brain size increased.

This went on for nearly another billion years. There were natural disasters and mass extinctions. The creature best suited for survival of these cataclysms was a mouse-like creature with about 75 million neurons in his brain.

Then, 50 million years ago, while still mouse-like, you developed an opposable thumb, which made it possible for you to grasp. With this ability came dexterity. With dexterity came coordination and balance

This coordination and balance gave you the ability to grow larger. The dexterity to grasp twigs became the dexterity to grasp branches and live in the trees. Your eyes developed to see distance and precision, which allowed you to move from branch to branch with ease.

Then the forest cleared and gave way to the savannah, so you began to walk upright. Now your entire neuromuscular system has been charged with the maintenance of this upright posture. With your legs fully extended, your trunk supported vertically, and your head put on a swivel atop your spine, you are the first and since only fully upright animal on the planet. You have a wide field of vision, you can carry heavy objects in your arms, and you can walk and run efficiently for a long period of time. You can also sit upright, which frees your hands and arms to build tools and shape the world in the way you see fit. To support these functions, your neuromuscular system has grown to work in a completely new way.

Your brain used the neurons that developed from tool-making and creativity to perform other tasks. One of those was the communication through sounds. You could now work with your fellow tribe members to create consistent sounds to denote various concepts in the environment.

This allowed you to think about your environment in more complex ways, work together, and survive.

At this point, no other species on earth even comes close to your intellectual capacity.

Then you used this language to communicate with the fairer sex. It's a good thing, too, because women are a challenge—much more of a challenge than your natural environment. Your final neurological growth spurt occurred to appease her needs—not only her communicative needs but her emotional and physical needs. You began to have sex more often, and for pleasure—mostly for the female's pleasure. This sexualization of the female made her needs insatiable. Her insatiable needs selected for quality males and so your advancement was accelerated, even when the environment didn't demand it.

She demanded you love and appreciate her, too. This not only made your brain larger, but it made your testicles smaller, which made it even more likely you would adapt through manipulation of the environment, rather than overcome it by brute force.

At this point, the brain of your children had become too big to fit through their mother's hips at the end of gestation, so they were birthed prematurely. This made them helpless for the first two years of life, which required you to stick around after their birth to help take care of and provide for them. New, crucial relationships formed, and so your brain became even more complex. The nuclear family is born.

Then about 300,000 years ago, maybe before, your brain reached a point at which it is as developed as it is now—about 100 billion neurons—all of which you acquired from the oxygen use, mate connection, dexterity, vision, coordination, balance, touch, creativity, language, and socialization.

Your brain created by these practical abilities became larger than the sum of its parts, and you were able to use it in ways unforeseen by your evolutionary demands. You began to think abstractly—you connected similar experiences and ideas, which caused you to create explanations for your world. This accident of evolution has become your most powerful tool for adaptation and survival.

Then, on a morning like any other, for reasons as mysterious as why you crawled up on land, you turned one of these abstract thoughts back on yourself. You may have wondered why you can move your arm when you think to move your arm. You may have wondered why there are other animals that look similar to you, and what it means that you look different. You may have eaten some plants that allowed you to see the same old reality in new and profound ways. You may have even begun to wonder who you were and what you wanted to do with your life.

You were confused as to why you asked such questions, let alone by the answers. You furrowed your brow and gave an inquisitive look, and you uttered something in your Paleolithic tongue that roughly translated to, "Wait... what the hell?"

And so we have self-awareness.

The Self-Awareness Uncertainty Principle

Self-awareness is necessary for change and growth, as you've already learned. But if your last four billion years on this planet is any indication, it has often been sufficient for change and growth. The more you are aware of, the more your psychology must change to keep up with your awareness. This is a phenomenon I call the Self-Awareness Uncertainty Principle.

It's like the Heisenberg Uncertainty Principle, which is a concept in quantum mechanics that states the nature of matter changes simply by our measurement of it. The same is true of yourself—you invariably change when you merely see yourself.

It's rare to come across a case in which somebody has seen themselves for what they are, acknowledged it wholeheartedly, and not gone on to take steps to change and grow. Sometimes the shock of the awareness causes psychological debilitation in the short-term; but once they accept reality, they begin to take the steps to improve. And they do it almost unconsciously, as if there's a drive for more life—ie individuation—built into man (four billion years of evolution demands this drive), and all he must do is see himself for what he is to activate it.

Here I'm reminded of the story of how David Hasselhoff got sober. He was an alcoholic for years because he's an 80s TV star, but one morning his daughter turned a camera on him as he was drunk, and he later saw the video. For the first time, he saw his drunkenness for what it was, not for how it felt to him through the prism of his lies. When he was drunk, he felt like he looked awesome, but turns out he would hit himself in the head with cheeseburgers. After his awareness expanded, he made the commitment to do everything he could to become sober, and he did.

In a sense you could say he was aware of his intoxication before this—after all, he was the one who poured the Lowenbrau down his gullet for breakfast—but when he saw the video of himself drunk on camera, he was able to see himself through a clearer lens, no pun intended.

Part IV: Self-Awareness

The SAUP explains why we cannot trust weight loss studies. Prior to the experiment, scientists weigh and measure the participants. Simply by being weighed and measured, the participants lose weight automatically. Most of us are fatter than we think we are, so when we see how fat we are in reality, this tends to compel us, often unconsciously, to make the necessary changes to lose weight.

The awareness of "holy crap, I cannot believe how fat I am!" makes us lose the weight we need to lose, regardless of the diet the scientists put us on. This is why yoga pants, a seemingly benevolent if not stupendous invention, ultimately make girls fatter. When a girl's clothes expand with her waistline, it will be more difficult for her to become aware of her expanded waistline.

This is how to think about your self-awareness in that it will make the pain of it more bearable. To see yourself for what you are is how to grow.

A story from my life

I did a comedy show at a club one night and they offered to record my set for free. Comedy clubs give you free stuff when you're not good enough to be paid in money. Afterward, while viewing the video, I barely paid attention to my set because I couldn't get over how fat I looked. People say the camera adds ten pounds. But the camera doesn't add ten pounds; we only think we're thinner than we are. After that, I didn't make a specific plan to lose weight, but over the next few months I lost 15 pounds. All it took was awareness. This is how actors can stay thin even though they're notorious partiers.

Self-awareness may be a magic pill, but it's a magic pill that tastes like cod liver oil. Even with what I know about self-awareness and what it can do for you, I still crumble to a pile of rationalizations and cowardice when faced with more awareness. When we become aware of something we've done wrong, especially if it has occurred for a while, we want to hit reset on life. We have fantasies that involve a return to our five-year-old self so we can live life over again with this newfound awareness.

The point is that self-awareness is a revolution. No revolution is fun while it happens, but eventually the revolution pays off, and the country is free to live again—at least until another revolution is necessary.

Anger and Anxiety: the Main Barriers to Self-Awareness

Remember from *Identity* that anger and anxiety are packaged information—files in the subconscious, too many files to look at all at once, all of them with the same, general message. You feel the barometric reading of those files as either "I can't" for anxiety or "I need" for anger.

In other words, your anger and anxiety are bunched up information in your mind. This is information about yourself and the world. To see that information you have yet to see is no different than to read a book about World War II that you have yet to read. It makes sense you would lack awareness of World War II if you never looked at it. The book is too heavy to lift and nobody else reads it so who would care? This invariably impedes your awareness of World War II because the book contains information outside of your awareness.

When anger and anxiety are unconscious, they distort reality and effectively short-circuit our brain. We disconnect from the facts to satisfy the latent emotions.

This is a phenomenon similar to politics, as I discuss in my article, *The Politics of Your Mind*.

Men are political beings, which means we will often put the interest of our group before facts. Our group could be any group—an ethnic group, family group, college group, or it could mean a political party group.

Facts are great, but sometimes they get in the way of what our group wants, and we let our political natures win in order for the group to survive.

In the same way, our mind becomes political with itself, you could say, when we lack awareness of an emotion. The emotion tends to take precedence over awareness—ie over the facts of reality and of ourselves. Rather than look at facts that may trigger an emotion, we look for facts that confirm whatever emotions are in our awareness.

Where groups are present, we inevitably dissociate from the facts. When latent emotions are present, we inevitably dissociate from the facts. It's how humans work together. It's how we work with ourselves.

As we use groups to work in our favor to master external politics, so too must we use emotions to work in our favor to master internal politics.

To do this, we feel an emotion and we accept it. We neither control it, nor do we let it control us. Rather, we use the emotion as a guide to mature, win-win action. This is what I describe in *Anxiety* and *Anger*.

As Perseus tames Pegasus, as a dam tames a river, as Daniel Plainview tames an oil well, we tame emotions. Only then are we able look at the emotion for what it is. Only then are we able to use emotions as guides for action, as a guide for self-awareness. Emotions are zip files filled with truths that reason alone could not discover, and they can be used to act in ways reason alone could not conceive.

The healthy psyche is nourished by this integration of reason and emotion, these supposedly disparate parts of our mind.

Therefore, the more we are able to recognize and manage our anger and anxiety, the more self-aware we will necessarily become.

Our pathway to self-awareness isn't impeded by emotions, rather by emotions we do not identify. We come up with ways to rationalize our emotions, even when we don't know we're doing it. Self-protection is the antithesis of self-awareness.

This happens when a guy is "friend-zoned" by a girl. One girl gives him even a smidgen of affection, and so he pines and yearns and supplicates to her in the hopes that maybe one day he will date her. He thinks he pines out of desire, but in truth he does it out of anxiety—he pines as a result of his fear of loss. His mind has folders packed with files that say he's unattractive, which creates anxiety ("I cannot get a girl to like me"), so this one girl who is friends with him must be the answer to this Gordian Knot. Only once he manages his anxiety, which turns his "I am incapable" files into "I am capable" files, does he see his pines for this girl only at the command of his anxiety.

This perceptual distortion of reality is the cause of cognitive biases, which we will talk about next.

Cognitive Biases

A cognitive bias is a tendency to think in a way that warps our perception of reality, and of ourselves. Our mind doesn't perceive reality as it is, but as we want it to be. Our perception of reality doesn't satisfy the demands of reality, rather the demands of our latent emotions.

The idea that our mind can shape reality is a relatively new one. It was popularized in *Prolegomena to Any Future Metaphysics* by Immanuel Kant, the most influential philosopher of the last 200 years. Before Kant, it was thought that our mind only perceives reality; that our mind only conforms to the facts of reality. Kant's insight, however, was that reality conforms to the facts of our mind.

This became known as the Copernican Revolution in philosophy. Copernicus figured out the earth revolved around the sun, which changed the way we saw ourselves, and the way we saw our place in the universe. Similarly, Kant changed the way we think about man's relationship with reality.

However, Kant was only correct in a certain context. It is true our mind shapes reality, but it's not literally true, as Kant thought. Our mind doesn't shape reality—it only shapes our perception of reality. Hence a cognitive bias.

When we understand Kant's insight to be figurative—as psychologically true, not philosophically true—and when we understand the mechanism behind it, we can understand how to overcome cognitive biases and perceive reality correctly. (Otherwise, we could say our idea of a cognitive bias is a cognitive bias, the paradox of all subjectivism.)

So below is a list of the fundamental cognitive biases, and how to overcome each one as explained through the three previous books on the unification of psychology—through the confrontation of anxiety, the assertion of anger, and the fortification of our identity.

There are more cognitive biases than what I list here, but most of them are glorified restatements of the main biases below. Or they only describe human peccadilloes, which do little if anything to impede self-awareness.

Confirmation bias: This is the mother of cognitive biases, the one that feeds most of the others. This is when we only pay attention to the facts of reality that fit our view of the world, rather than create a worldview through the integration of the facts of reality. It's the politics of the mind, as we discussed. This is what most people do, which is why they lack awareness, which is why they never grow.

To fix: The best way to overcome confirmation bias is to use your anxiety and anger in mature ways. When we force the facts to fit our worldview, we use the facts to fit our emotions. We're more likely to do this when we are unaware of latent emotions that control our life. The more we can introspect and uncover nuggets of anger and anxiety in our psyche, and the better we assert the anger and confront the anxiety, the less we will be susceptible to confirmation bias.

Status quo bias: This is the tendency to prefer the current state of affairs as opposed to another state, even if the other state would be more favorable. In other words, we seek what we're used to. This is why girls who were abused by their fathers get boyfriends who abuse them the same. This is why most people are born and die in the same social and economic class. It's why we stick with a career even though it doesn't make us happy. It's what we're used to, it's what our brain is used to, so that's where we remain. Status quo bias is what David Foster Wallace symbolizes in his *This Is Water* speech—a fish doesn't know what water is because it's all around him.

To fix: The status quo of our mind is an emotional state. It is a state we are comfortable with, even if it doesn't feel good. As with the healthy management of confirmation bias, we need to manage anger and anxiety to overcome this bias. At least we need to chip away at the anger and anxiety to be less affected by status quo bias. Status quo bias is the result of our boundary as well, since a boundary is only a manifestation of how we manage emotions. We may have implicitly accepted a boundary to be middle class because we grew up middle class. But when we introspect and figure out where this boundary (re value) comes from—or what it is based on within our psyche—then we can set a new boundary, and so buck the internal status quo.

Information bias: This is the tendency to seek information when it cannot affect our decisions or the impact of those decisions. I mention this bias because it's what young and cerebral men succumb to when they're trying to improve their lives. I know I did and still do. We think the more we learn about psychology, the more mature we'll become. So we may sit in our rooms all day with our face in a book, which of course quickly engenders diminishing returns. As much as the truth of psychology will transform your life, there's a limit and even a hindrance to information without action.

To fix: Information bias is a form of compulsive behavior, which is the result of avoiding loss, or anxiety. So to overcome information bias, manage anxiety.

Illusory truth effect: We tend to believe something if it's been repeated often, whether in our own minds or in popular culture. Rich people are mean, men are the oppressors of women, hard work pays off, and your vote counts. These generalizations become our worldview, and then through confirmation bias, we only pay attention to the facts that support that worldview.

To fix: The reason we go along with what gets repeated isn't because we begin to believe these illusions as true, but because we don't want to stand alone. Latent anxiety says it's a threat to stand alone, and our weak boundary says we're not strong enough to stand alone. Manage anxiety and firm up the boundary, and we'll be in a much better position to question dogma, specifically the dogma of our own beliefs.

Rationalization: This is similar to confirmation bias, but rather than find facts that support our latent emotions, we fabricate facts to support our emotions. The common example of a rationalization is when we call a girl a bad name for breaking up with us in order to appease the anxiety of the loss.

To fix: The first step to reduce rationalization is to manage anger and anxiety, as we would to reduce confirmation bias. But since rationalization involves an extra lie, it's imperative to firm up your boundary specifically through honesty, a topic I will discuss in the next chapter.

Bias blind spot: This is the tendency to recognize cognitive biases more in other people than in ourselves. Not to blow sunshine up your butt, but if you're reading this book, you probably do have fewer cognitive biases than most men. That being said, you're probably a young guy, and testosterone doesn't make you smart. It makes you awesome, but not smart.

To fix: It's easier to see your blind spots when you have a strong boundary. Men typically don't want to see their blind spots because to admit blindness is to admit weakness. Of course, we don't mind an admission of weakness when we ultimately see ourselves as strong, and to see ourselves as strong we of course need to strengthen our boundary.

Exposure effect: This is the tendency to like something you have been exposed to more often than not. You won't find a lot of Gator fans from Alabama, or a lot of NASCAR fans in the Northeast, or a lot of hockey fans in Mexico. There's no rationale for this, except that we unconsciously accept what's around us, even if it's through mere exposure.

To fix: The exposure effect is another way to say fear of change. Manage anxiety and we'll be more able to deal with loss, which is always a part of change.

Semmelweis reflex: This is the tendency to disregard facts, ideas, and information that contradict well-established systems of belief. The Semmelweis reflex is, therefore, the inverse of confirmation bias.

To fix: The Semmelweis reflex stems from the fear of change. The fear of change is, as we just mentioned, ultimately the fear of loss, and so it boils down to anxiety.

Denial: This is the tendency to block out uncomfortable realities of life. There are those secrets we only tell our close friends, then there are those secrets we never tell anyone else, then there are those secrets we keep even from ourselves. This is what denial is—a cover up of facts, even from our conscious awareness.

To fix: The key word there is uncomfortable. Denial is the result of discomfort with discomfort. As we become more comfortable with uncomfortable emotions, then we'll be less susceptible to denial. The more we manage anger and anxiety, the less likely we'll fall victim to denial.

Conclusion: Kant thought men necessarily warp reality based on what they are, but the truth is we only have a proclivity to warp reality. Similarly, we have a proclivity to eat too much candy until we gain weight—but simply because this drive to consume sugar is a part of who we are doesn't mean we're destined to be fat. We can become aware of the processes by which we get fat and change our behavior accordingly. It may take effort and regulation, but it's possible.

Likewise, it takes knowledge and effort to see reality for what it is, and to see yourself for what you are.

Composure
So far we've only talked about awareness of our life in general. But there's another element to self-awareness that involves awareness in real time. It's to be aware of our thoughts and actions even as they occur. The extent to which we can be aware of ourselves in real time is the extent to which we can handle tension.

We've all been in important and so stressful situations, like a pay-raise negotiation. We become too nervous and lose a sense of ourselves. We say things we don't mean to say, and we do things we don't mean to do. We fumble ideas and stutter through our words. Then after the meeting, we look back to how we acted and think, "What the hell happened?" What happened is we lost our composure, and we did it because our psychology wasn't equipped to handle the tension in the moment.

Specifically, this occurs when we lack the confidence to handle the anxiety we feel, we lack the compassion to handle the anger we feel, and we lack the necessary boundary to understand or delineate the situation. As a result, we are overwhelmed with anxiety, anger, or weakness (or all three).

The first step to handle tension is to notice when the tension from the environment is too much to bear. Notice why we lose composure and notice what we need to work on in our psychology as a result.

This is the gold in the loss of composure—we will look like a dork, and oh boy will we feel like a dork, but the loss of composure exposes what we need to work on in our psychology. If there ever were "gimme" points for self-awareness, composure loss is it. It's a bulldozer that plows through our mechanism for self-protection right into the truth of what we are.

It doesn't matter how cool we pretend to be, if our voice squeaks on in the presence of a girl and then we become too nervous to ask for her phone number, it's difficult to hide from that.

When NFL players talk about their first year in the league, they remark how fast the game seems compared with college. But after a few seasons, their mind acclimates to the speed, and they begin to be more aware of themselves and the other players on the field. They are more aware of themselves in real time. This is because they learn to handle the tension of their emotions and identity as players. As when we get our see legs, their mind adapts unconsciously.

A new level of anxiety comes up for rookies when they encounter faster change on the field. A new level of anger comes up for them when they encounter greater needs. A new level of weakness comes up for them when they encounter deeper complexities of what it takes to understand an NFL playbook.

Part IV: Self-Awareness

To handle tension and keep your composure is what it means to be in the present moment. The present moment is the pilot light of psychology, because it's only in the present moment we can make a decision, and it's only with a decision that we can confront anxiety, assert anger, and strengthen our boundary.

Therefore, the loss of composure bridges the gap between the theory of what self-awareness is and the practice of how to develop it, which we will cover next.

Chapter Two: Practice

How to Become More Self-Aware

"Live as if you were living for the second time and had acted as wrongly the first time as you are about to act now."
– Viktor Frankl

Honesty

Honesty is inseparable from self-awareness. In fact, this part could well be called *Honesty*. But honesty is the process, self-awareness is the result.

Every lie we tell is one more message we put in our mind that says, "We can fake our way through life"—ie "We can disconnect from reality, other people, and who we are." To disconnect from reality is to lose self-awareness.

Even small lies damage our ability to see who we are. The problem with small lies is they work. They feel good in the same way it feels good to look at yourself in a funhouse mirror that makes you look thin. We know it's not real though it still feels good. And the comfort of the small lie unconsciously steers us toward bigger lies. People who see themselves as thinner than they are in a warped mirror, even if they know it's warped, are more likely to eat junk food afterward when given the choice.

When we lie about the small stuff, we lie about the big stuff.

Perhaps the most destructive result of dishonesty is it cuts us off from other people. Healthy relationships are, as we will see, essential for self-awareness.

The One Rule for Becoming Honest

The only way I have known to become more honest is to put a standing order in the mind to be honest once per day in a situation where we would have previously told a lie. Imagine we're out with a girl and it comes to a situation where we would've lied about how we make more money than we do. We probably wouldn't explicitly lie about how much money we make, but we may imply we make more than we do. In that situation, we purposefully tell the truth, the whole truth, and nothing but the truth.

(Simply say, "I don't have a lot of money, which I consider as part of my charm.") And that's all we need to do, once per day.

I've seen junkies—ie professional liars—become some of the most honest people I've met within the span of several months through no more than this simple rule.

When we're honest about the small stuff, we're honest about the big stuff.

When we follow this rule, we find we'll be more connected with the world, and we will naturally begin to be more honest. As small lies steer us toward big lies, small truths steer us toward big truths. We will become more comfortable with the truth, and therefore less comfortable with lies.

If we ever get off track and begin to lie again, it's no big deal—simply go back to the One Rule. It's a simple way to overcome the most formidable barrier that stands between us and psychological health.

The Bonus Rule for Becoming Honest

If the One Rule isn't enough, then we may need to employ the Bonus Rule, which is to write down past lies, or any lie that bothers us, and tell them to somebody. This may take several tries because, if we're a champion liar, it will take a while for all the lies to come into our conscious mind. The good news, however, is we can come clean about the lies to anybody—it doesn't need to be the person we lied to. You can talk to a bum on the street about your lies, as long as he's at least half conscious. This hits the reset buttons on dishonesty, which may be necessary if we've been dishonest for awhile. And it will make it more natural to employ the One Rule.

As important as honesty is, it's difficult to be 100 percent honest—if not impossible. Sometimes we simply cannot know whether we say something because it's true, or because it fits an agenda. But this is no different than the admission we're never going to be 100 percent self-aware. Incorporate the habits that tend toward honesty, and let what happens happen. We'll head in the right direction—I know this for a fact.

Now is when you expect me to say that sometimes we can lie when it comes to important situations where we lie would mean to save a job or a friendship. But I won't ay this. We're susceptible enough to unconscious dishonesty that there's no room in psychological health for conscious dishonesty. Without at least the intent of honesty, any attempt to become self-aware will be in vain. Learn to communicate harsh truths in an appropriate way—ie learn to be kind and humorous with the truth—then learn to manage the short-term damage caused by the honesty, and you'll be amazed how honest you can be. You'll be even more amazed by how life becomes more fun and successful.

Conclusion: Self-awareness is a garden we always prune and revise. Honesty is how we sharpen the shears. If the shears are dull, any attempt to work on the garden will be in vain at best, and counterproductive at worst.

Indications of Poor Self-Awareness
It would be repetitive to delineate the signs we lack self-awareness. Immature management of anxiety and anger, and signs of a weak boundary, are ultimately all indications we lack self-awareness. Furthermore, it's safe to assume we lack self-awareness in every area of our life that could be a lot better—whether the area is money, relationships, girls, family, or career.

However, there are a few additional and less-obvious signs we lack self-awareness. One sign of poor self-awareness, which we mentioned in the previous chapter, is the loss of composure. A loss of composure occurs when we lack the confidence to handle our anxiety, we lack the compassion to handle our anger, and we lack the strength to handle our weakness. So we are overwhelmed and lose a sense of ourselves in the present moment.

It's natural to want to avoid a situation that causes the loss of our composure, but that situation is our best friend. It means there is latent anxiety or anger we have not regulated and handled. Seek out these situations as often as possible. The more we become triggered (and then accept and take responsibility for our emotions), the more self-aware we will become.

A loss of composure says something about us, not about our environment.

Another sign we lack self-awareness is when seemingly inexplicable things happen to us. I once met a guy who said he'd been mugged three times in the past six weeks. From the way he told the story, I could tell his attitude was one of disbelief: "How could anybody be so unlucky?" he thought. But it was clear from a two-minute conversation with him that he projected weakness, which criminals pick up and prey on accordingly.

A less obvious sign we lack self-awareness is when time seems to fly by. This indicates something besides us is in control of our life—that we're only a spectator. It's a slow death and we feel as though nothing can be done about it. We feel vagueness and confusion.

Repetition of behaviors and thoughts, or autopilot, often occurs with the flight of time. Though, as mentioned, these signs of poor self-awareness stem from unmanaged emotion, a weak boundary, or both.

What's more important is knowing how to increase self-awareness, which we will cover next.

Techniques to Increase Self-Awareness

There is no finish line for self-awareness, as there is no finish line for confidence, compassion, and strength. These are processes we work with though we never achieve perfection. So if you sit around and wait for a sign you lack self-awareness, then you lack self-awareness. Remember, self-awareness is like a scientific theory. When Darwin formulated the theory of evolution, scientists didn't wait for people do disprove it, they went to work to collect evidence, a constant process to verify what fit the theory and expand its permutations beyond what Darwin could have conceived.

Here is an exhaustive list of what we can do to expand self-awareness. I suggest you try all the techniques but only practice the ones that work for you. After a while, come back to the ones that didn't work initially, and you may be able to give new practice to them. Self-awareness begets self-awareness.

Write Down Negative Beliefs and Fears

It's painful and therefore helpful to write down all of our negative beliefs—negative beliefs about us and about the world, other people, politicians, and institutions. If we can think about it, then we can think negatively about it. Under this umbrella of "negative beliefs" live our completely irrational and unsolvable fears, so it's good to write those down, too.

As I've complained about elsewhere in this book, it's become sacrilege in modern psychology to be negative, but negative beliefs and fears only hurt us when we're unaware of them. It may feel bad to see the recesses of negativity there in front of us, but let's take solace in the fact that when we see them on that sheet in front of us, we're aware of them. And it's only when they remain latent do they remain powerful. As is hopefully gathered by now, it's amazing how often misery and self-awareness overlap.

Here, I'll list my fears to show you it's not the end of the world.

I'll never make enough money to live what I consider to be a full life.

I'm going to go bald, which will be bad for me because I'm not tall. It's okay for guys taller than six feet to go bald. But for short guys, it's a bad look, because then you're short *and* bald.

I'm going to break up with my girlfriend and never be able to hold down a relationship, which is what I really want, and it's what would ultimately make me happy.

Similarly, there's a self-destructive impulse that ruins my life. It may lay dormant for years, but I fear there's an innate dark spot there that may come to the surface and take over.

I can never be truly self-aware, so I will continue to make mistakes I cannot see. and I will never be able to see. My life will stagnate, and it will do so completely outside of my awareness forever.

I'm a little brother, so I fear I have this little brother affability that endears me to people, but it keeps them from taking me seriously. There's nothing I can do about it because I'm a little brother.

I may be intelligent, somewhat, but intelligence doesn't mean much unless you can connect with others, and I have a difficult time with that. I fear I may never be connected with others in the way I want to be. I fear I may become homeless as a result, forever focused on my psychological theories. Honestly, that still sounds like a pretty good life, and think I may inherently be a loser because I'm surprisingly okay with homelessness. It's an ambivalence I have toward success. A part of me wants to be homeless—it's like a latent homosexual, except I'm a latent homeless guy.

See? That wasn't so bad, but we'll stop it there (I could keep going). But as we put this stuff on paper, we realize how silly it is. Every time we do this, these negative beliefs and fears become less powerful. They may not end here, but as we become aware of them, their impact on life wanes. We're above them as we write them out and so look down on them rather than unconsciously hold them over our head.

Now do me a big favor and don't tell anybody about this list.

The Lame Mirror Technique

This is a technique I steal from Nathaniel Branden, and it's a variation of the above technique. Here is how it works: Look at yourself in the mirror—a bathroom mirror works but a full-length mirror is preferable. Look into your eyes as you say, "I like myself." (Now you know why I called it the *lame* mirror technique.)

After you say "I like myself," notice what protests your mind comes up with in response to this statement: "You cannot like yourself, you're going bald;" or "you cannot like yourself, you're not living up to your father's expectations;" or "you cannot like yourself, you haven't had sex in four months;" or "you cannot like yourself, you always stay up late to watch dumb action movies and Facebook stalk girls you went to high school with."

It's the natural state of the human to like himself, so the point here is to be aware of what's in our subconscious mind that disfigures this natural state. The lame mirror technique unearths these thoughts and feelings so we can see them.

Once these uncomfortable thoughts come to the surface, it's good to write them down on a piece of paper as in the previous "write down fears and negative beliefs" technique. When we do this, we take the nebulous thoughts of our subconscious—thoughts and beliefs that may have sabotaged decisions for years—and make them concrete and observable. From here, we can use what we've discussed in *Anxiety, Anger,* and *Identity* to maturely manage whatever baggage comes to the surface.

A variation of the mirror technique is to imagine yourself with a beautiful woman—a woman who you would think is way out of your league. Probably a girl you saw on the train earlier that day but were too afraid to talk with. Like the mirror technique, note the protests your mind comes up with when you imagine yourself in bed with her, preferably with her consent. This is something you'll probably imagine anyway, but now you can do it in a way that increases self-awareness.

Yet another variation of the mirror technique is to imagine yourself in your ideal career. Imagine yourself as you work and give orders. Imagine how people would respond to you. How would they talk to you? How would you talk to them? How would you feel about yourself? What would you wear? Then notice the protests that surface in your mind.

It's important to remember that, when we employ these techniques, we don't create new protests—these protests were already in our mind, beneath awareness. When we imagine ourselves in these situations, we uncover them.

Record Yourself

Record yourself in conversations. This will reveal aspects of who you are that you would never pick up on your own, nor would you pick up from the all the "honest" feedback from a therapist, girlfriend, or friend.

To listen to yourself is an excellent way to view yourself objectively, and so be as honest as you possibly can be with who you are. It gives you the opportunity to ask yourself, "What would I think of this guy if I were to meet him and hear him talk for the first time?"

We will get the most insight into ourselves when we record us in a normal circumstance, like when we're at dinner with friends, and then in a tense circumstance, like a sales call or a business negotiation. The former provides a baseline feedback, while the latter provides feedback when we're most vulnerable. It's no different than a stress test.

Also, keep in mind it's illegal to secretly record a conversation in most states. So be sure not to get caught.

Travel

Travel is mostly overrated—it's glorified looking, as I call it. But something unique happens when we remove ourselves from our routine—we gain perspective on the routine. Travel removes us from our life existentially, so it tends to remove us from our life psychologically. This makes it easier to look back on ourselves more objectively. I have found an occasional uproot, even to a ranch in the boonies for the weekend, puts me in a state of mind amicable to awareness, and I'm more able to make the next adjustments, whatever I think they may be. Whenever I have come back from a trip, I have made at least one adjustment to my life that ended up being significant down the road. When I plop back down on my sofa, I look around and think, "Oh yeah, what the heck was I doing here anyway?"

Seek to Understand the Irrational

The cliché is it's better to understand than to be understood, but it's true. Whenever we come across a belief or idea we don't understand—especially one that seems completely ridiculous and irrational—it's important to challenge ourselves to understand it. When we understand a belief that is incorrect, we're in a better position to see us for what we are since it strengthens the ability to look beyond our mere perceptions to the conception of what something is. This doesn't mean all truth is relative and all beliefs are equally relevant, but even if a belief is wrong, it's still important to understand it.

A story from my life

I'm an atheist, so it's a beloved pastime of mine is to tell religious people how stupid they are. Hey, who needs friends? But even if I am right about the nonexistence of God (and I am), this doesn't help me, and it doesn't help people who believe in God. What I eventually did, as my belligerence subsided, is realize, through the guidance of Jung, "Hey, most of the people on earth, who are all biologically similar to me, believe in God. So there must be something to the idea, even if it's not a guy in the sky." It turns out there is something to the idea of God, which has a lot of overlap with my theory of the subconscious, which I elaborated on in Identity. *This one idea has done a lot to connect me with readers, even atheists. I understand humanity better, and I understand myself better. What's more, I don't see religious people as beneath me, even if they are wrong (which they are). In many ways, I can see how theists are better than I am. In fact, though I still consider myself an atheist, now I may be an atheist with an asterisk. All it took was for me to limit my obsession with the perceptual truth and begin to understand.*

**Listen to someone else as if it's true,
then ask yourself what it's true of.**

The more perspectives we have, the more likely we are to use those perspectives to suss out blind spots in our own life. Each new perspective, each new system of belief, is a new lens we can use to see who we are. We understand others so we can understand us.

Build Relationships

The channel through which self-awareness flows originates from others as well. This occurs when we build relationships and so we're able to see other people see us. This is called psychic objectivity. Though the psychic objectivity will only be proportional to the extent our relationships are healthy—that is, open, honest, and mutually beneficial. Hopefully we're not too surprised to learn this involves mature use of anxiety and anger. To put this idea another way, the more honest we can be with ourselves, the more honest we can be with others, the more others will be able to see us for what we are, and so we can experience psychic objectivity.

Limit Distractions

A distraction could be any one thing that removes us from our life and problems—ie our emotional issues. This usually takes the form of frequent internet use, television, alcohol, drugs, and consumerism. Nothing wrong with fun, but if we use the fun as a distraction rather than an enhancement, it's no longer fun—it's not un-fun, which is a big difference and limits awareness.

Meditate

Sit alone, in silence, and move as little as possible. It's preferable to stare at a wall, or anything else that will tune out the senses. This allows our thoughts and emotions that are typically outside of aware-ness to come into awareness. Think of your mind like a jar of water with a scoop of dirt in it. When you're unaware, it's like shaking up the jar, which creates a dark cloud in the water. When you sit in silence, the dirt settles to the bottom. When the dirt settles, this alone will reduce stress and make you more aware. But the purpose of meditation isn't only to let the dirt settle, it's to scoop the dirt out. This is the difference between stress reduction and clarity about the source of the stress so we can figure out what we need to do to remove the dirt ie stress (either what anxiety to confront or what anger to assert).

An example from my life
Here's what happened in my life, that never would have happened, if I didn't meditate: broke up with a toxic girlfriend, went to grad school, built a relationship with a girl who was a better situation for me, got kicked out of grad school, and unified psychology. I wouldn't say I have the most spectacular life, but when I look back on it, especially the last ten years or so, I think there's no way this life could have been anyone else's. It's totally mine because all of my decisions came from me, from my anger and anxiety, and from my own values. Meditation made this more likely to happen.

A good start would be to meditate for 20 minutes, three times per week. But I find it more helpful once you go past 20 or 25 minutes. Sunday mornings, I will sometimes sit for an hour. Since, as the nature of our psychology indicates, the purpose of meditation isn't to control our thoughts—rather it's to get in touch with our issues—two questions to ask as we meditate are: What am I avoiding? and What do I need? Issues come to the surface, the mind is more clear, and we're in as much control as we ever will be.

Journal

Most guys have a difficult time with journaling at first, especially since it often doesn't begin to pay off for a few months. To get through the growing pains of journaling, I recommend, at the end of each day, to write down two things you did well that day, and two things you didn't do well, how it's your responsibility, and what you could have done differently. I still use this format when I don't know what to journal about, and it's still helpful. This is a practice in honesty. Or, if you feel up to it, go through the introspection steps for any particular challenge you faced throughout the day. You remember them? That's right, 1 identify the emotion, 2 identify why you feel the emotion, 3 identify what makes this emotion personal, 4 ask yourself if you're correct, 5 take responsibility, and 6 summarize what you learned, and your next step.

As you take stock of your day, you begin to notice your patterns of behavior and unconscious loops. You can begin to see yourself as a rat in a maze. The hum of awareness makes us ever more likely to do what we need to do to create the appropriate changes in our lives.

Dream Analysis

I've read everything Freud and Jung, and then some, have said about dreams and dream analysis. This is a cherished topic for me so I could go on for pages or volumes about it, but if I had to sum up what I think I know about dream analysis, it would be to simply ask yourself what a particular dream wants you to do. That's it. For any dream, impactful or otherwise, we can draw a beautiful mind kind of diagram of connections and analysis, but ultimately I think the best way to analyze the dream, and so gain self-awareness, is to ask yourself what a dream wants you to do, then do that thing. See what happens as a result. Remember: Make. More. Decisions.

Therapy

Therapists cannot manage your anger or anxiety, they cannot solidify your values, and they cannot make your decisions. Only you can do that. But they can do something to make your sessions priceless, which is to help you become more self-aware. Therapists know more about psychology than you do—theoretically, at least—so what the therapist can do is listen to your experiences, then relate back to you how he sees them through his prism of knowledge and intuition. Quality therapy is like the Mirror of Erised from Harry Potter—it doesn't show you how you appear; rather what's there beneath the surface. As such, it's a catalyst for every one of these self-awareness exercises.

Image Consultant

The problem with therapists is they will rarely be honest with you because they believe there's a distinction between honesty (even gentle honesty) and helpfulness. So what I often recommend for a different perspective—if not a better one—is to get a consultation with a personal stylist. Sometimes he's called an image consultant, which is a lame name but in any case he's helpful. He has a fine-tuned intuition to read people, and we pay for the honesty of this intuition. It may devastate us when he says we look like a computer programmer who hasn't seen a vagina since his mother's on the day he was born, but devastation is another word for self-awareness.

Sentence Completions

This is another exercise I steal from Nathaniel Branden. It's excellent for unearthing thoughts, beliefs, and emotions that are just out of our awareness. Take a prompt from Dr. Branden's comprehensive list of sentence completions (search for it) and write down a minimum of seven responses to each one. The key is to do it without analysis, as fast as you can, which guarantees the process taps into parts of your subconscious where the light of your conscious barely shines. Sentence completions are a modified form of journaling, and they can be used in place of journaling if you want. My favorite prompts are:

"As I am five percent more honest today…"
"As I live five percent more consciously today…"
"As I assert my needs today…"

"As I feel my anger today…"
"As I confront my anxiety today…"
"As I feel my anxiety today…"
"As I am five percent more connected today…"

Dr. Braden's insight to work on only the next five percent of psychological growth is powerful. That's all you need to do. And really, one percent would be more than enough. He knew that the first five percent is the most difficult—from here, the next one percent is a little easier, then the next is easier still. As long as you do it every day, the improvements will come easier and faster than you ever would have expected—that's the nature of compounded interest.

"What Am I Thinking Now?" "What Am I Feeling Now?"
When all else fails, ask yourself these two questions at any time or in any place to become more aware immediately. They snap you back to reality when you lose a sense of yourself. As soon as you ask yourself whether you're aware, then you're aware.

Conclusion: Ultimately, self-awareness comes from discomfort. When we're uncomfortable, we see those parts of us we were previously unaware of. That is why a situation is uncomfortable—it is the unknown, it is outside of awareness. The more we peer into those recesses, through the employ of the above exercises, the more self-aware we will become.

Chapter Three: Application

Psychology Unified.

"Concision in style, precision in thought, decision in life."
– Victor Hugo

Now that we have completed the unification of psychology, let's draw from five of my past clients to demonstrate how the pieces of psychology fit together.

NOTE: *I'll put my comments in this format to connect the cases to my theory.*

Phil Makes Amends

Phil is 63 years old. By all accounts, he is successful. He has a job he cares about, he has a girlfriend—it's taken him a while to get to this point, but he's made it. Though he has had off-and-on insomnia for decades, and he has a tendency toward OCD, no official diagnosis has been made.

NOTE: *Prolonged insomnia is caused by latent anxiety, 100 percent of the time. It's often thought depression is the cause of insomnia, but depression is the result of insomnia. You have a need for sleep that's not being met, and you don't know how to get it met. Stored up anger collapses into sadness, and chronic sadness becomes depression. So with anxiety at the root of insomnia, that's where we begin. That may not be the main problem, but it's as good a place as any to start.*

So I wonder what may be the cause of Phil's anxiety, which will be either a loss or threat of loss, or it could be a threat Phil chronically avoids. After we dig some, he reluctantly reveals he has an ex-wife who he treated poorly. The relationship ended badly, and he hasn't seen her in more than 20 years. We talk about what happened, how it's his responsibility, and what he may still be avoiding.

NOTE: *This is the process of emotions we discussed in how to build your subconscious. When we talk about our anxiety in a way that connects us with others, as we take responsibility for it, we dislodge it from our subconscious, so to speak, which it easier to see and so use. Without this awareness, anxiety becomes fossilized in our mind over the years. In order to do anything conscious with it, we need to loosen it up. This is best done* by feeling the anxiety, and feeling the anxiety is catalyzed by when we talk about it in a healthy way.

Phil still is reluctant to admit he experiences anxiety or avoids the situation. Then I ask him to imagine what he would do if he saw his ex-wife walking down the street toward him. He immediately shot up, "I'd run to the other side of the street!"

It becomes clear to Phil what he needs to do—call his ex-wife and express true remorse to her. Not to explain his behavior or make excuses, but to amend the situation as best he can. Phil is reluctant to do this, so I took him through the exposure therapy steps I discuss in *Anxiety*. He wrote out what he wanted to say (at least the main points) and rehearsed the conversation with me.

NOTE: *As Phil becomes aware of his anxiety, he sees how the anxiety is manifested in the files of his subconscious. He sees the "I can't" thoughts in the form of "I can't confront my wife." The implication of this thought is "I can't manage relationships with women." When Phil sees this, even implicitly, he firms up his boundary, which makes his decision to call his wife more obvious, and therefore easier.*

Phil resisted: "This is exactly how my father treated my mother, so it's what I'm going to do, too."

NOTE: *I've seen this kind of reasoning (or more specifically, rationalization) from every single one of my clients. Every single one. I don't blame them, and I don't blame you when you do it (though I do blame myself when I do it). But let's be clear: healthy management of anxiety, or any other branch of psychology, is no different than learning how to climb a mountain. If you had trouble on a mountain climbing expedition, you wouldn't excuse yourself with, "Sorry, but my dad wasn't a mountain climber, and he never taught me how to climb, so I'm not going to learn now." Instead, you would ask the guide what you could do to improve, and then you would do it. The only difference is we know little about psycholo-*

gy compared to mountain climbing, so we are less aware of the definitive ways to improve our psychologies. That is, until now.

So Phil calls his ex-wife, who last he heard lives in Switzerland. He gets her sister on the phone and she tells Phil that his ex-wife has Alzheimer's, and she doesn't even remember who Phil is anymore. She barely remembers who she, her sister, is.

Phil tells me about this and how he fell into a sharp depression marked by frequent bursts of tears over the next three days.

NOTE: *When Phil's ex-sister-in-law tells him his ex-wife doesn't even recognize his name, this shuts off the entire area called "ex-wife" from Phil's life. It effectively closes up this part of his boundary for his ex-wife, a boundary that had remained weak for more than two decades. Phil, in essence, has received a big "no" from his environment. (We know his boundary was weak because he was incredibly sensitive to even the idea of accidentally running into his ex-wife on the street.) Phil then experiences depression because he has a need to apologize to his wife, a need that can never be met. His anger overwhelmed him due to this impossibility, and it turned into depression.*

Phil decides he can still assert his need to apologize if he writes a letter to his ex-wife, puts in words everything he wants to say to her. He does so and tells me about what he wrote. With his boundary strengthened, he is able to put more energy into his relationship with his current girlfriend. He plans a trip to Europe with her. By our last session, Phil's insomnia and OCD behaviors begin to ameliorate.

Dean Replaces his Daughter

Dean is 47-years-old; he has an ex-wife who died of breast cancer and a daughter. He's become increasingly sad over the last several months because his daughter, his only child, will leave for college soon. He has a difficult time with the fact that he'll soon come home to an empty apartment.

NOTE: *Dean anticipates an imminent loss, which is the cause of anxiety. But with loss comes an unmet need, so anger and sadness are also present. Some men will tend to experience more of one emotion than the other. The reason for this is temperament, which is part of the unconscious and so we cannot change, but we can affect how our temperament plays out in life. How much can we affect the influence of our temperament? No one knows for sure, but I do know for a fact it's enough to make life a lot more happy and fun.*

I sense sadness predominates in Dean—he's lethargic, subdued—so I ask him what he needs. He chuckles as he says he needs his daughter to stay with him in perpetuity. He chuckles because he knows it's a ridiculous need to have. So I come to my own conclusions about what Dean needs. When I ask him about the last time he's been on a date, he says he doesn't date much. He works a lot, and he tries to spend the rest of his time with his daughter. Plus, he makes a point to mention—though sheepishly—he doesn't make a lot of money, or not as much as he used to make, and so (he says) he doesn't have enough money to go out with women.

Dean does make decent money as a real estate agent, but he used to be a hedge fund manager. He made millions but lost it all due to, as he puts it, "poor management, market fluctuations, and oh yeah my violent alcoholism." He's been in and out of recovery for 15 years, but as of our sessions, he hadn't had a drink in two years.

Part IV: Self-Awareness

Two weeks after I ask Dean about his love life, which he initially dismissed as irrelevant, he brings it up to me and is flabbergasted by how long it's been since he's gone out with another woman.

"Another woman besides your daughter," I say in an attempt at fun.

"Yeah, that's what I thought, ever since you mentioned it. My daughter has been the female relationship in my life. Maybe I'm not upset because my daughter is about to leave; I'm upset because I don't have anyone, and I don't feel like I could get anyone since I lost all my money."

NOTE: *Dean doesn't even consider going out with another woman— ie opening his boundary to that possibility—until he begins to psychologically let his daughter out of his life (to firm up his boundary for her) and let her make her own life (which allows her to develop her own boundary). Dean's story is an excellent demonstration of how our boundaries affect the boundaries of others. When we make our boundary healthier, this tends to make the boundaries of those around us healthier. It's also important to note that if you asked Dean prior to this realization if he was afraid of women, he would have dismissed it with a scoff. But he was afraid, deeply afraid—only he wasn't aware of it. Regardless, it still affected his behavior and how he perceived reality.*

Dean expresses doubts about going out with women because of his lack of money. I ask him if he would lie to a woman about how much money he made. He said he may not lie explicitly, but he would make it seem like he had more than he did. Especially at his age, according to Dean, it's sad when a man hasn't made a good sum of money (and held onto it).

I tell him that he will tend to lie about parts of his life where he feels uncomfortable (where he has a weak boundary), so when he goes out with women, he would pretend that he has more money than he does—which he could probably do because he inherited what sounds like a sweet apartment when his father died.

Dean has inherited a lot from his father. He was handed the hedge fund job on a platter through his father's connections, and his first wife seemed to only want him for his money. She left him and their daughter as soon as the money ran out. I conjectured she must have been a drug addict. Dean confirms she was.

NOTE: *Of course she was. Mothers don't leave their children unless they're on drugs. The point is Dean's done very little on his own. So to date a new woman isn't about dating a new woman, it's to do something on his own.*

I challenge Dean to be honest about his finances when he's out with women. He uses Tinder and Match to set up his dates, which I discourage but it's a step in the right direction for a guy who's been out of the game his entire life.

NOTE: *Dean has become more aware of his emotional issues—he's begun to feel his sadness, and so he's in touch with what it tells him he needs. The awareness of sadness has turned it back into anger, which has given a new intensity to Dean's eyes. His awareness of the sadness also causes him to solidify his values. Dean is now in the throes of huge growth, and all it took was a little nudge of self-awareness.*

Dean goes out with a few women though he lies to them at first. This causes frustration, which he tells me about.

NOTE: *As you begin to improve in one area of your psychology, your behavior probably won't change right away, but you will become upset with your old behavior. As the anger builds, you will be more likely change your behavior—ie do what it is you need to do that's in line with your now expanded self-awareness. I get a lot of emails from guys who say they're frustrated with themselves after they read my material, and my thought is, "good."*

Dean's old behavior is no longer acceptable to him, so he begins to be honest with women.

NOTE: *Dean's anger—his frustration with himself—drives him to confront his anxiety, which is rooted in his dishonesty about his lack of a stellar financial situation—or at least a financial situation that belies his apartment. The anger was needed to push him to confront his anxiety. As I wrote about in* Identity, *anger drives you toward a goal, and anxiety keeps you away from a goal. This push of anger and pull of anxiety tipped in favor of Dean's anger when he solidified his boundary through experience with women. It got him in touch with what was important to him, and so what he needed to do. When his need becomes more clear, his decision to act will be more definite. This will eventually lead him to get his need met, which is an honest relationship with a woman.*

Dean does begin to be honest with a woman, and he reports to me that she barely cared about his financial situation. This one shift in thought, and so shift in behavior, produces a major change in Dean's affect. He's a new man.

By our last session, Dean finds a woman who he likes and who he's honest with. It's too soon to tell if she's right for him, but the head fake is he learned a woman could want to be with him without any ulterior motives. More importantly, Dean for the first time considers what he wants out of a relationship with a woman. His daughter has moved out, now at college, and Dean feels a sense of relief that he can now have a healthier relationship with her.

NOTE: *Through honesty, Dean has strengthened his boundary, which made the delineation of what he wants in a relationship much easier. Once we strengthen our boundary in one area, it becomes easier to strengthen our boundary in another area.*

Gavin Becomes Homeless to Avoid Recovery

Eight months ago, Gavin was a one-percenter. He had a three-bedroom apartment in the East Village, a wife, two kids, and a dog. Now he's in a homeless shelter. What happened?

To protect Gavin's identity, I don't use his real name of course. But he does have an Irish name. So yes, alcoholism happened.

Alcoholism isn't a disease in the typical sense, but it is a compulsive behavior, so it does feel like a disease—something wrong with you completely outside of your immediate control. And as we remember from *Anxiety*, compulsion is caused by latent anxiety. Therefore, alcoholism is ultimately caused by anxiety.

Gavin has avoided much of his anxiety for more than 20 years—ever since he graduated high school. But in the past year, his imbibition began to escalate. He became aware enough to recognize what the whiskey did to him, but he avoided any sort of action to do anything about it. This increased his anxiety, which led to more serious benders. He knew he needed to go to treatment, but he was too afraid of what people would think of him if they knew he had an alcohol problem.

NOTE: *The anxiety that caused Gavin to drink also kept him from treatment because of the threat of loss of social status. This is typical of anxiety—it often gets in the way of the proper management of the anxiety.*

One day, about eight months prior to my work with Gavin, he made the resolution he would go an Alcoholics Anonymous group after work, but he never did because of what he thought would be a loss in his reputation, not only with others but with himself. This one act of avoidance was the tipping point. This is when he truly began to feel helpless, and so he began to drink even more than before, at least a fifth every day. He skipped work, which he never did before, and he was barely around for his wife and family.

Part IV: Self-Awareness

Gavin's wife was able to see what was happening because her father was an alcoholic (funny how that works), and she confronted him about it, so he punched her in the face. He doesn't remember it because he was blacked out. So she got scared and took the children and the dog to her mother's in Boston. Gavin spent the next two months in a veritable blackout. He didn't lose all of his money, but because of legal issues, he lost access to it and his apartment.

When Gavin ended up in a homeless shelter, he began to attend AA and started to look at himself. He did his fourth and fifth step of the program with me, which allowed him to talk about his trauma and anxiety—that which was the cause of his compulsion to drink.

NOTE: *This isn't an endorsement of AA, but the program has some benefits. While 12-step can be a gateway to mindlessness, it can also get the addict to look at himself and thereby become self-aware, which is an irreplaceable first step. It's like if you were the manager of an assembly line, and one day a machine broke down. It would make you feel helpless if you checked and couldn't figure out why the machine was broken. Then when you finally realized there was a piece of scrap metal jamming up the machine, you would feel capable again, a huge sense of relief, even before you were able to remove it.*

NOTE: *Gavin still has a lot of work to do. He has become aware of his emotional issues, but until he begins to manage them effectively, they will seep back into the recesses of his subconscious and he will feel the urge to drink again. However, simply through the placement of his trauma on a sheet of paper was a huge step in the right direction. Gavin looked at himself, and simply the knowledge of what drove him to drink lessened the compulsion to drink. Yet none of this could have been possible if he didn't first confront his anxiety through the open admission that he had a problem. Remember, the anxiety files—or the "I can't" files—in your mind can only control you if you're unaware of them. And you can only manage* them once you are aware of them. *Awareness solidifies your boundary, because now you're more aware of what you can do and what you cannot do in regard to your emotions. To see who and what we are is difficult, but it's half the battle.*

Morty Talks to his Son

Morty is a 76-year-old retired professor who has lived in the Upper West Side since he graduated from college. He sought therapy because his wife has recently become paralyzed due to a neurological disorder, and she's probably going to die within the year. We talk about the imminent loss and what Morty could do to cope with it.

NOTE: *Difficulty with loss is a function of anxiety, yes, but it's also a function of the boundary, or the inability to let a problem go that we cannot control—in this case, the inevitability of death. Contrary to popular belief, about 94 percent of people begin to handle the death of their spouse within six months of the death. They're still sad, but they adapt and move on. Those who do not move on and grieve perpetually have a fundamental anxiety issue that's triggered by the loss of their spouse.*

From what I can tell, Morty doesn't seem to have a serious anxiety issue—his wife will die and he will be sad, but there's no reason to believe he will struggle any more than others do when they lose their spouse.

Rather than deal with his dying wife, I'm more interested in the fact that Morty has a son who hasn't come to the hospital to see his mother, and Morty has from the same son two grandchildren who Morty isn't allowed to see. According to Morty's side of the story, it's because his son is "a fucking asshole." This may be true, but I work with Morty to understand he may be at least partially responsible for the situation. Unless someone is on drugs, they wouldn't cut off a family member like that.

NOTE: *As we discussed in* Anger, *it's rare to be met with unprovoked hostility, especially on a consistent basis. If someone is hostile to you, it's appropriate to defend yourself at first; but when you have a moment, it's helpful to ask what you may have done to provoke the hostility. Remember: "listen to someone else as if it's true, then ask yourself what it's true of." This isn't to blame Morty, as he accused me of initially. This is only to recognize hostility for what it is, and to notice how it affects relationships. The point is to do everything we can do to turn our hostility into a healthy assertion of our need.*

I send Morty a record of our session, and he's surprised to find out how "cantankerous" (his word) he sounds. Then, when he meets his son for lunch, which he does every few weeks, he records the conversation. Again, he is surprised how cantankerous he sounds. This is Morty's latent anger that expresses itself as hostility—a cantankerous affect always is. The hostility is a turn-off to his son, and his son and his wife are new-age Manhattan parents who don't want their children to be around any negativity or "bad vibes," which may be myopic of them, but that is their right.

NOTE: *Morty initially recoils at the idea that he is responsible for his inability to see his grandchildren, but luckily for Morty, he really wants to see his grandchildren, so he has the impetus to accept reality for what it is. It's no fun to hear we're responsible for any situation in life that's not going well. In fact, this aversion even shows up in the academic world: merely implying someone may be responsible for their situation is a faux pas in psychology programs. It's seen as "blaming the victim," when really, on a psychological level, no one is to blame—the point is only to increase awareness.*

Morty and I work together to see what he could be angry about, and that's when he tells me how it upset him greatly when his son married his daughter-in-law, because she's not Jewish. However, he never said anything because he knew it was wrong for him to take issue with her race.

NOTE: *Though it may be wrong for Morty to take issue with his daughter-in-law's race, it's impossible to put anger in a box. It seeps into actions and thoughts, outside of our awareness. Remember, our emotion is always justified, but what we do with our emotion is not always justified. Because Morty saw his emotion as unjustified, it was difficult for him to accept it as his, so he was unable to use it in a mature way.*

So Morty meets with his son and talks to him about the misgivings he has about his daughter-in-law's race. We work out how he can express his misgivings in a way that connects with his son as he takes responsibility. It feels good for Morty to get his anger off his chest in an appropriate way, and it opens up new pathways of communication between him and his son.

NOTE: *Morty thought his need was for his daughter-in-law to be a Jew, but this need was immature because it decreased his pain rather than increase his pleasure. In truth his need was to see his grandchildren. His self-awareness changed his identity, which made his need more appropriate for his environment. This made it more natural for him to get his need met and therefore reduce his anger. Through a discussion with his son about the race of his wife, Morty was able to integrate a healthy expression of his anger into his boundary, so he was able to connect it with his son and the rest of his family. This connection of disparate or disavowed parts of ourselves to others and our identity is what people mean (whether they know it or not) when they use the term "spirituality."*

NOTE: *Morty had an anger issue, yes, but it was partly based on a boundary issue. The expression of his need to his son, and the comprehension of how he turned his need into hostility, allowed him to become more aware of himself. This made it much easier to firm up his boundary through the decision to talk to his son about his anger. It also showed him how silly it was for him to be concerned about his daughter-in-law's race. This can be Morty's value, I make no judgment about that, but it's clearly not his son's value, so it's beholden to a healthy boundary to accept it.*

Lance Bounces Around

Lance is retired. Retired from what no one knows. He's bounced around most of his life, taking odd jobs to make ends meet, which hasn't been too difficult for him because he inherited an apartment from his family in a building that has its own Wikipedia page. But Lance was never going to have his own Wikipedia page because he never needed one.

He worked as a piano tuner for a while. Then as a golf instructor. He worked in advertising, which is the general-issue industry for a man who doesn't know what to do with his life. He never married, and he never had kids. He was too busy with what he needed to do to get by.

Without my direction, he brings up his high school days. He was "bullied" a lot, to use a favorite word of his when he describes himself.

NOTE: *I get the sense Lance enjoys the fact he was bullied. He's had trauma, and he likes his trauma. This is typical. When you've experienced an issue for years, like the view of yourself as a victim, then you like that issue, even if it doesn't feel good. It's the aforementioned status quo bias. Your brain is accustomed to a certain emotional state, so it does what it can to perpetuate that state, even to the detriment of your life.*

Lance has his reasons for his failure to launch. He had a difficult childhood, and that's what he will focus on. I ask him what he needs; he said he needed a better childhood. I asked him why he needed it; he said without a decent childhood, there was never any hope for him. He's a dabbler, and he's a dabbler from New York, so he knows enough about psychology to justify his life.

I ask him about women, he says he's not interested. I ask him about what he's interested in, and he mentions about 35 different things, none of which are the least bit interesting. He buys honey from Ohio in five-gallon jugs, which works out to be a great deal. He swears by short-grained rice and sardines. He brags to me that he's never had to buy furniture because he always gets it from the curb. When you live in a part of New York that's littered with multi-millionaires, you find nice furniture on the street.

NOTE: *Lance is, in effect, a drug addict. He has sabotaged his life to experience the precise concoction of anxiety and sadness he experiences when he thinks about his childhood and adolescence.*

I ask him how much porn he watches, he shifts in his seat and says, "every so often." This is code for "all the time."

I ask him about his finances, and he says they're good because his head is above water.

NOTE: *Lance has it figured out from his perspective, so it's difficult for me to get through to him. He has his hobbies, his health food, his NPR, and everything else a comfortable man could ever want.*

I talk to him about his boundary and how a lack of it could explain why he wastes his time and mine by talking about bargain honey. He tells me he's heard about a boundary before, and it sounds like a nice theory. I challenge him that he has a weak boundary, and that his life would be much better if he strengthened it. He would get clear about who he is, and he would lessen the focus on what happened to him in high school, more than four decades ago.

But Lance isn't interested. He only came to therapy because he had ten visits covered by his health insurance.

NOTE: *The lack of need is worse than the lack of satisfaction. Without a need, there is nothing to do, nothing to overcome, no anger to assert, no anxiety to confront, and no life worthy of awareness. From what I can tell, the number one problem that faces men in the comfortable West is there is no problem. No incentive. No impetus. No urge. But without a boundary there can be none of these forces. And without awareness, there can be no boundary. Lance's life would have been infinitely better if he would have simply picked something like honey farming, even if he didn't like it that much, than pick nothing at all. That one decision could have been the cata-*

lyst of his psychology—he could have strengthened his boundary (thereby clarify his anger), managed his adolescent trauma, and had many opportunities to confront his anxiety. So in the interest of a strong boundary, let's use Lance's story as a warning and wish him well.

Conclusion: Self-Awareness

A dynamic psychology is a healthy psychology.

When we confront anxiety, if strengthens our identity. And because our identity is the nexus of psychology, it affects our anger and self-awareness.

Likewise, when we assert anger, it strengthens our identity, which in turn exposes and clarifies anxiety. Each part of psychology is connected to identity, and each part, when managed, enlightens the other branches.

This is psychological health: the movement of our libido from one branch to the next. Each branch receives the energy from the previous one, and uses it in the next right way.

Though sometimes our energy gets stuck on one of the branches of psychology. I've seen clients who have been stuck at anxiety for decades. With no confrontation of their anxiety, their identity withers, their anger retreats and grows.

It's the role of self-awareness, therefore, to give our psychology the proverbial kick in the butt.

Imagine yourself boxing with your psychology, self-awareness is like the jab. You use it to keep your psychology on its heels, never let it get too comfortable, never let it become too complacent. When your psychology exposes a vulnerable spot, that's when you come in with a cross from your dominant hand. This would be a decision to confront your anxiety, assert your anger, or strengthen your identity.

The jab is the foundation. It isn't flashy. It doesn't make the girls swoon. It won't knock anyone out. And it seems much easier to execute than it is. Every beginner thinks they have the jab mastered by the end of their first week. But the pros know it's impossible to master the jab. Like self-awareness, when you think you have it just right, your psychology becomes used to it, and you need to evolve—as you have been for the last four billion years.

Conclusion: The Unification of Psychology

The world's oldest profession is neither prostitution nor politics, as it's commonly believed. The oldest profession is shamanism—the shaman's job is to remove our consciousness from our body so we can rise above it, which gives us the ability to look back on it and see what we are. Then we are reintroduced to ourselves with new knowledge and an expanded range of consciousness.

What we have in *Man's Guide to Psychology* is the first fully-integrated approach to shamanism. It's taken 30,000 years, but there it is.

There were false starts and misguided attempts. The scientists *disintegrated* psychology; they told us the disparate parts of our psyche were understandable, but at odds with each other. The id and super ego would forever be in conflict; a traumatic childhood was something to be explored and understood, but never overcome; anger about our father was always about the inevitable difficulties of the father-son relationship, never about anger. Life, therefore, was something to be endured.

The religionists *misintegrated* psychology. Though they offered a complete picture of psychology, it was conceived by supernaturalism, by truths without basis in reality. The mind was noble but ineffective in this world; emotions were inherently irrational, only to be avoided through the submission to duty and asceticism until the escape from their tyranny in death; actions were either good or evil, never a step in the right direction. Life, therefore, was something to be mastered.

Yet life is neither something to be endured, nor is it something to be mastered—it's something to be enjoyed. There is no perpetual struggle, there is no combination lock, and there is no finish line. We build our lives, neither with a sense of meaninglessness, nor with a sense of self-satisfaction. One block on top of the other, according to a self-made plan. Each decision makes us more excited to be alive—each success allows us to yearn for more.

To Be Continued…

There it is—combined with *Anxiety, Anger,* and *Identity,* you have for the first time the unification and integration of man's psychology.

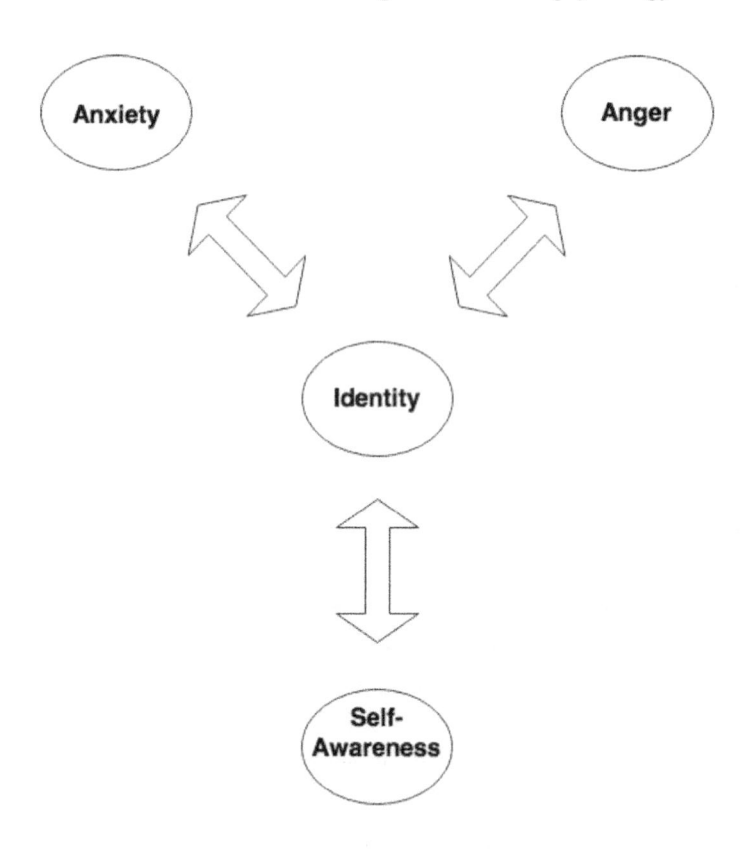

```
    Anxiety                           Anger
        ↘                             ↙
              Identity
                ↕
            Self-
          Awareness
```

While *Man's Guide to Psychology* is complete, it's not comprehensive. These ideas will require elaboration for the same reason E = mc^2 requires elaboration. But what's contained in this book is a foundation—a *Prolegomenon*, you could say—to any future psychology.

Even if I'm full of ten times more crap than I think I am, the ideas I've laid out here are a big deal. I know it's ridiculous when I compare myself to Plato in the introduction; and to Einstein and Kant like I just did there. Maybe I am ridiculous, but my ideas are not. So thank you for being part of their inception.

About the Author

Mark Derian is a PhD dropout in psychology.

Schedule a free consultation: joinanimus.com/schedule

Printed in Great Britain
by Amazon